History & Reminiscences
of the University of Georgia

History & Reminiscences of the University of Georgia

Vince Dooley

Paintings by Steve Penley

Looking Glass Books

Published by Looking Glass Books, Inc.

Distributed by John F. Blair, Publisher

Jacket and book design by Angela Harwood

Manufactured in Canada

ISBN: 978-1-929619-45-0

"Vince Dooley and I both came to UGA in 1963. Over the years he was highly successful as football coach and athletic director while I published a good bit on the history of the old school. Now he is doing it too in this interesting, lively, and very personal run through more than two centuries with special emphasis on our own time on campus—almost half a century! New paintings in color by Steve Penley reinforce this useful addition to the growing collection of eyewitness reminiscences of a booming American university."

— F. N. BONEY, UGA professor of history, emeritus
Author of *A Pictorial History of the University of Georgia* and *A Walking Tour of the University of Georgia*

"Vince Dooley's book is yet another excellent example of his prolific research and authorship abilities. His thoroughly interesting composition on the history the University and a number of its most famous leaders and students is absolutely fascinating, and to me it was extremely informative. In addition, his coverage of events over the last forty-five-plus years was spellbinding and very enlightening, especially his own involvement and perspectives. I enjoyed every word of it, and I enthusiastically recommend it to everyone, especially those who have been connected in any way with the University."

— NICK CHILIVIS, UGA Law School, 1953
UGA Law School adjunct professor, retired
UGA Research Foundation Board and UGA Foundation

"Coach Dooley's athletic legacy is secure, but as author and historian, he's creating a literary legacy that's just as important and influential. Vince Dooley and the University of Georgia are inseparable, and in telling the story of the University's history, he explores his own past as well. This book is the story of a great University, but it's also part autobiography, and all of it is fascinating. It's all here, too, from Abraham Baldwin to Michael Adams, and Coach Dooley pulls no punches. Like all good historians, he doesn't just recite facts, he inteprets and analyzes the past, giving us a history of the University and its people that is like life itself, lived day by day: rich and complex, good and bad, tragic and inspiring, not always easily understood. As a student at Georgia's flagship university during some of Coach Dooley's best years, I can attest that here he has given all of us who love this great institution and what it stands for a great gift. Seize it."

— STAN DEATON, PhD, Senior Historian, The Georgia Historical Society
M.A., UGA, 1988
A.B.J., UGA's Henry W. Grady School of Journalism, 1986

"Coach Vincent J. Dooley provides vignettes and reminiscences in this new tome that umbrella the history of The University of Georgia. Baldwin, Meigs, Church, LeConte, Ward are brought to life in the brilliantly conceived, accurately documented, and passionately written narration of this great University. The difficult and best of times are brought to the surface. Financial fluctuations, leadership, foibles, political imbalances, wars, integration, academics, and athletics are symbiotically meshed into the history of this world-class Institution. This is not a staid, static, or torpid account, but a living, breathing, metamorphic convergence of facts, thoughts, ideas, and experiences. The result is a wonderful textual journey, engineered by a renaissance thinker who doubled as football coach and athletic director for forty years. Coach Dooley's love for the University of Georgia is deeply embedded and unwavering. In the last paragraph, he states, 'I still bleed red and black and always will.'"

— MICHAEL A. DIRR, PhD, UGA professor of horticulture
Former director of the (UGA) State Botanical Garden of Georgia

"With a serious and multi-faceted bent for history, Vince Dooley offers illuminating insights into the University's past and present (including his era as football coach and athletic director). If he had not become a football coach, he would have flourished as a history professor. If Georgia hadn't beckoned him to coach, a PhD was likely. If the sis-boom-bah enrapturing moments accented by the falling leaves were his first choice, his second most favorite place to be would be the library. From this book, you can conclude he had to have spent a lot of time there, anyway—enjoying it to the fullest."

— LORAN SMITH, UGA Journalism School, 1962
UGA track team captain, 1960
Bulldog historian, columnist, and author

To the thousands of alumni, past and present,
and the dedicated professors, staff, administrators, and supporters
who made this great University and all that it represents.

CONTENTS

History & Reminiscences
of the University of Georgia

Franklin College (later Old College), modeled after Connecticut Hall at Yale

$\mathscr{B}$EGINNINGS

Abraham Baldwin

Though I have spent almost five decades of my life associated with the University of Georgia, little did I know that the institution indirectly touched a part of my life from the beginning. Growing up in Mobile, Alabama, I spent most of every summer across Mobile Bay in adjacent Baldwin County. This Alabama county ironically was named after Abraham Baldwin, a Yale graduate who more than any single person was responsible for founding the University of Georgia.

I never connected this Alabama–Georgia oddity until many years after accepting the head coaching position at the University. I was on a football recruiting trip in Bay Minette, Alabama, which is Baldwin County's seat. I read the historical marker at the courthouse describing the county's origin and its being named for Abraham Baldwin of Georgia. After the initial shock, I soon discovered, with further research, most of the original citizens of the county had come from Georgia. They had such high regard for the gifted Baldwin, they named the county in his honor two years after he died in office as a United States senator. The county was actually established in 1809 while it was part of the Mississippi Territory, ten years before Alabama

Abraham Baldwin

state and the nation, it was his contribution in founding the University of Georgia for which he is most remembered. Baldwin had always been keenly interested in education, and through his connections with then-Georgia governor Lyman Hall, also a Yale graduate, the General Assembly in 1784 set aside 40,000 acres of land from Washington and Franklin counties to endow "a college or seminary of learning."

Baldwin, who was elected as a trustee to the college, drew up the school's charter using the Yale charter as a model. He then lobbied the other trustees and the legislature to adopt the document. Thus, on January 27, 1785, the Georgia assembly adopted the charter making the University of Georgia the first chartered state university in the nation. Baldwin was named its first president. Actually, he became president in name only, for it took sixteen years for the charter he drew to be implemented and for the school to officially open. During that stretch of time, Baldwin had busied himself with politics while the trustees of the school struggled to accumulate funds from the endowed 40,000 acres. Finally, at the turn of the century there was some six thousand dollars in the coffer, and the decision was made to select a site for the institution.

Once again, Baldwin, who by then was a United States senator, assumed a prominent leadership role chairing a five-man committee to select a site in the interior of the state "free from the miasmic fevers of the coastal areas." The committee, travelling by horseback, selected a land site on a hill near the Indian Territory in Jackson County (later Clarke County), close to the headwaters of the Oconee River. One of the committee members, John Milledge, who later became governor of Georgia, purchased and gave to the trustees 633 acres surrounding the selected site. The town that would arise from the site was appropriately given the name Athens, and the Classic City was born.

On September 12, 2011, thanks to the initiative of Dr. Loch K. Johnson, Regents Professor of Political Science in the School of Public and International Affairs and funding support primarily by the UGA Alumni Association, the University dedicated a bronze statue to Baldwin. The life-size (plus one half) statue is located in front of Old College facing north toward downtown Athens.

became a state. Considering Baldwin's contribution to the University, the nation, and to their native state, those early pioneers paid a fitting tribute to this early icon.

Baldwin had entered Yale College in 1768 at the age of fourteen and after graduation studied theology. He later became a chaplain in George Washington's army during the revolution. Baldwin later studied law and moved to Georgia at the age of twenty-nine to start a practice. He entered public service in the state legislature and later led the Georgia delegation to the Constitutional Convention in Philadelphia, where he played a significant role in drafting the United States Constitution, becoming a signee. Baldwin served in the U.S. House of Representatives until 1799, when he was elected to the United States Senate, where he served until his death in 1807. For all his contributions to the

Josiah Meigs

The College Becomes a Reality

Choosing the site for the college was the last official act of President Baldwin, who passed the torch to one of his students at Yale, Josiah Meigs. Baldwin then turned his attention to the pressing duties of United States senator, while Meigs assumed the duties of president and professor, starting classes in 1801. Meigs often recruited students all over the state. Historian Thomas G. Dyer, referencing the Board of Trustees minutes, wrote that Meigs reported by "late 1803 that between thirty and forty-five" had enrolled. Considering the small numbers it is interesting there was not a more accurate count.

The curriculum consisted of the traditional classical studies. Meigs would teach either outside or in a log cabin until the first building was completed. There were ten in the first graduating class in 1804, and they received their diplomas in front of that first building, still under construction. The building, modeled after Connecticut Hall at Yale, became known as Franklin College (later Old College) in honor of Ben Franklin. Since the University was located near the Indian Territory, for protection the sheriff of the county (Jackson, later Clarke) led the graduation parade with a drawn sword. The tradition carries on today more than two hundred years later.

Meigs, a professed liberal who promoted science and mathematics at the school, eventually clashed with the conservative Board of Trustees. Adding to the tension was the school's financial struggles, exacerbated by poor support from the legislature. Enrollment was also in a steady decline. As struggles continued, Meigs was replaced, and is remembered today with the University's highest teaching honor in his name. The college continued to decline under the next two presidents, John Brown and Robert Finley, founder of the American Colonization Society. By 1819 there were fewer than twenty-four students, with the campus building in disrepair. Fortunately in those difficult times, the capable Moses Waddel, a Presbyterian minister, assumed the presidency and guided the school through the crisis. Waddel was educated at Hampden-Sydney College in Virginia, a historic and proud school that my son-in-law, Jay Mitchell, would proudly attend nearly two centuries later (Jay has often told me how "awesome" the school is). Waddel was a dedicated worker and travelled the state recruiting students, most of whom were sons of planters, politicians, and war heroes, all from the upper echelon of society. Waddel built the enrollment to more than a hundred by the time he retired in 1829. He passed the torch to another Presbyterian minister, Alonzo Church, who served for thirty years, the longest tenure in the University's history.

Alonzo Church and the Antebellum Years

Church was a conservative, headstrong disciplinarian who ruled the school with an iron fist, emphasizing, ac-

Moses Waddel

Church's Spartan culture had a profound effect, however, in dealing with the faculty. His old-school, uncompromising attitude resulted in the loss of some talented faculty members, including McCay, the faculty secretary and an outstanding teacher. Foremost among the departed professors were the famous LeConte brothers.

Joseph and John LeConte, native Georgians (Liberty County) as well as University and Harvard graduates and medical doctors, taught science at the University representing a new breed of teachers. Joseph LeConte wrote several essays during his three years at the University. The most noteworthy was "Classics vs. Mathematics," which called for "curriculum revisions that would provide better balance between the study of ancient languages and of mathematics . . . complemented by the study of science," according to UGA Emeritus Professor of History Lester D. Stephens. This progressive philosophy brought both Joseph and John LeConte in direct conflict with the conservative trustees along with the authoritarian and classical educational philosophy of Church.

In 1855 both LeContes left Georgia, and the loss of these prestigious professors and their philosophical differences with President Church became a public controversy. Several newspapers regretted the loss of the LeContes, with one inferring that "Church was responsible for driving out the LeContes and many other able professors. This caused Church to strike back with "fury" defending his policies, which in turn caused John to write that he was duty bound "to expose the lamentable frailties of the one who presides over my alma mater." The public verbal battles continued for months, with Church weathering the storm.

Eventually the LeConte brothers ended up teaching at The College of South Carolina (now the University of South Carolina), which, according to historian Stephens, "helped push that institution to the forefront of science in the antebellum Deep South." The LeContes remained at the institution until after the Civil War.

After the war the brothers desired to leave the devastated South. Since both had served the Confederacy in niter (chemicals for explosives) works, they knew their future would not be in the North. Thus, fortuitously for them and for California, they moved to the West Coast to become part of the initial faculty of the

cording to historian Thomas G. Dyer, "punctuality and exactitude." Despite the regimentation, there were student problems with drinking and disorderly conduct. Historian F.N. Boney in his pictorial history of the University wrote that "in 1840 six drunken seniors stoned President Church and Professor Charles F. McCay leaving both badly bruised." Undeterred, Church and McCay cut the students no slack insisting on law and order on campus.

Joseph LeConte

John LeConte

newly founded University of California at Berkeley. John later became president and Joseph a renowned botany professor at the new school. Both are memorialized with buildings named for them at the three universities where they taught.

At Georgia, LeConte Hall is the home of the history department (formerly biology), and a fitting tribute to each of the brothers is displayed in the entrance foyer of the building. A very large, excellent painting of Joseph also hangs in the same entrance hall. John, a preeminent entomologist, has a Georgia bird (LeConte's Sparrow) named for him. Joseph was held in such high esteem as a scientist and as a charter member of the

Sierra Club that an Alaska glacier and mountains in the Smokies and Sierra are named in his honor. Recent information, however, suggests Mount LeConte, the third-highest peak in the Great Smokies and located near Knoxville, Tennessee, was named for John instead of Joseph as earlier assumed. Despite the controversy, the mountain is a popular hiking site with a lodge located on its 6,593-foot summit. The LeConte brothers are the most notable of the many distinguished professors who have left the University through the years in response to sometimes authoritative, uncompromising University presidents.

The Arch, patterned after the Great Seal of Georgia

A Garden of Eden

There were other challenges during the long tenure of Church. During the antebellum years, tough economic times were always at the forefront of any crisis the school faced. For instance, the school tragically was forced to sell its first botanical garden. Located west of the campus, just north of Broad Street around Tanyard Creek and Finley Hill was a beautiful, several-acre garden with numerous plants and specimen trees. Some of the old trees are still standing in a yard once owned by Professor Malthus Ward, who established the garden. Several years ago, I visited the location on the corner of Dearing and the cobblestone Finley Street with renowned horticulture professor Dr. Michael Dirr and found magnolias, ginkgos, elms, oaks, and other old trees from the original garden.

The garden, which contained many rare and exotic plants, became the town's greatest attraction, with a national reputation. It was described by historian E. Merton Coulter as "a veritable Garden of Eden with hills and valleys, two sparkling brooks, a lake…and over two hundred plants, shrubs, and trees from all over the world." Harsh economic times dealt a death blow to this treasure that with better times and proper care today might well have been among the great garden parks in the country.

The property was sold in 1858 for one thousand dollars. The trustees used the money to plant more trees on campus and build a black iron ornamental fence that surrounded the campus at the time. The fence still encompasses part of the North Campus. In addition to the fence's ornamental qualities, it served as a barrier to the livestock that roamed the area in those days. The entrance gate of the decorative fence was patterned after the great seal of Georgia with the classic three columns. The free-standing gate, known as the Arch, remains today as the most famous symbol of the University.

Despite the lost opportunity in the antebellum years of having a world-renowned botanical garden, the University restored horticultural pride some 150 years later by the addition of a campus arboretum and the State Botanical Garden. Thanks to the trees that were planted hundreds of years ago, the University campus was designated as an arboretum with a mis-

sion statement of providing "a biological and aesthetic collection of trees, shrubs and herbaceous plants for the enjoyment and education of the students, faculty, staff and citizens of Georgia."

In 1968, 293 acres with winding trails along the Oconee River became the University of Georgia's botanical garden, the first since the ill-fated magnificent garden of the antebellum years. The garden, called "a living plant library," has been a learning laboratory for classes in botany, forestry, ecology, horticulture, and landscape architecture. In 1984 the garden was designated by the Georgia General Assembly as the State Botanical Garden of Georgia. Adding to the growth of the garden was a $3 million gift from the Callaway Foundation for a conservatory and visitors center. The latest addition to the garden proper was an international garden. Within the property and close to the garden area two significant buildings were added in the decade of the 1990s. The Deen Day Smith Chapel opened in 1994 and has since provided opportunities for contemplative services, concerts, weddings, and receptions. In 1998 the Garden Club of Georgia moved into a new building on the property, vacating the Founders Garden on North Campus where the first garden club in America was founded. President Church, who did not want to sell the original botanical garden, would be proud today of the State Botanical Garden of Georgia.

Literary Societies

The antebellum students described by Historian Dyer as "lively, rambunctious, contentious and occasionally violent…had a positive counterbalance in the activities of student-organized and student-managed literary societies."

Almost from the beginning of the University, literary societies became the foundation of the extracurricular activities. As was the case with most universities at the time, these debating societies became very competitive, developing strong rivalries.

Demosthenian, the first such society, was organized in 1803, shortly after classes started "for the purpose of…extemporary speaking." The society was named after Demosthenes, the prominent Greek orator and statesman of the fourth century B.C. He was their hero, and the members studied his life and speeches for de-

Demosthenian Hall

cades. The society held its meetings in an old school-room until Demosthenian Hall, a federal-style building, was completed in 1824. Up until that time, the society's dominance of the oratory scene caused most of its members to "grow lax and listless," but soon a new society was founded that stirred the Demosthenian's competitive juices.

In 1820 Joseph H. Lumpkin, a Princeton graduate who returned to practice law in his hometown of Athens, founded Phi Kappa, a secret literary society. Known only to its members were the words "Philo Kosmean" (whatever kind of love that means). Nevertheless, this underdog society became highly competitive, reaching its zenith in 1836 when it built a classical "hall of architectural dignity" across the quadrangle from Demosthenian Hall. The two societies engaged in lively debates, and for the most part their relationship was amicable. However, from time to time animosities arose between these two societies and lasted for years. The rivalry was intense, and the spirited debates offered a welcome diversion from the regimented routine of college life.

Both societies gradually gave way to other extra-curricular activities, such as social fraternities and intercollegiate athletics. Finally World War II brought to an end Phi Kappa, though there were periodic brief moments of revising the society. For many years the building was the office of noted historian E. Merton Coulter, and today the classic building is used as a computer training center. Demosthenians, on the other hand, continued their old debating traditions and yearly held all night sessions on various subjects.

For many years I gave the State of the Bulldog address, usually at 11:00 PM. Dean William Tate then gave the State of the University address at midnight. I would hang around many nights to listen to this icon, who served the University for some fifty years. Tate served as Dean of Men, and for twenty-five years single-handedly dealt with all discipline problems. Tate was an institution within an institution. I have met several hundred alumni who, for the most part, proudly recall they had been to his office for an unforgettable session. All spoke of Dean Tate with affection and admiration.

For decades Tate symbolized what the University of Georgia was. As a former track star he had an understanding of athletics and was a good supporter of our program. His knowledge of the University and his

counsel were a tremendous help to me, and I took advantage by listening to every speech he delivered.

I especially remember what was perhaps his last midnight State of the University address to Demosthenians. His health had faded in his retirement, and this particular time he was in the hospital but persuaded the doctors to allow him to leave for an hour to give his annual midnight address. I remember distinctly he wore a robe and had grown a short white beard that covered his face. I will never forget how he opened his remarks that night. He told the Demosthenians that his wife had come to the hospital yesterday and had given him the highest compliment he had ever received. She told him he looked just like General Robert E. Lee, whose portrait was hanging in the back of the upper chamber. The students roared, shaking the rafters of the old hall. General Lee, incidentally, had been offered honorary membership, which he graciously accepted.

The Tate Student Center was appropriately named for Dean Tate and will be a constant reminder of his service to the University and its students. His presence and voice of reason during integration and the Vietnam War in the 1960s and '70s calmed tensions among many unruly crowds that could have become violent. He is the epitome of the old saying, "They don't make them like that anymore!"

As generations of distinguished Demosthenian alumni pass, they continue to hand off the torch to young members who keep alive some of the great traditions of the society. Every year in February (around the birthday of the society) the members still hold the all night session with debates and informed lecturers. Currently, however, no one is carrying on the tradition of delivering the midnight State of the University address like Dean Tate. I am sure that if Dean Tate were giving the State of the University Address during the latter years of the Church administration, just prior to the Civil War, he would not have been able to paint a very rosy picture.

The End of an Era

The controversy surrounding the resignation and dismissal of the LeConte brothers, along with Church's conflict with other faculty members, was at the fore-

Andrew Lipscomb

campus to "prepare" and be "tutored" to enter the upper classes that would study at Franklin College. It was a sound plan but was never effectively executed. A new mode of student discipline based on demerits was also instituted. In addition, a law school emerged off campus in 1859, thanks to the initiative of Joseph H. Lumpkin and his son-in-law, Thomas R.R. Cobb, who held classes in their law office.

Another reform measure called for the head of the campus to carry the title of chancellor, spending most of his time travelling the state promoting the University. The president, in turn, would run the campus on a daily basis. Fortunately during these times of changes, Andrew A. Lipscomb proved to be an excellent choice as the first chancellor. His modern views on education instilled optimism that the University was about to emerge as a modern, progressive institution of higher education. However, the excitement generated by Lipscomb was tempered as the nation began to deal with its greatest crisis.

Civil War and the University

The bitterness that had built up for decades between the two sections of the country erupted in 1861 soon after Abraham Lincoln was elected president. While he received the necessary electoral votes, he received only 39 percent of the popular vote, making Lincoln the most minority president ever elected. The election featured four candidates running under various tickets. South Carolina seceded from the Union immediately, followed by six other Deep South states including Georgia. After Georgia seceded, the state virtually became a separate country for a short period of time before joining the Confederate States of America. In February 1861, even before Lincoln was inaugurated, Jefferson Davis was sworn in as president of the Confederacy in Montgomery, Alabama, its first capital. In the words of the fire-eater William Lowndes Yancey of Alabama, "The man and the hour have met."

At the convention in Montgomery, former University students were prevalent. Eight of the ten delegates sent by the state of Georgia had their training at the University. Foremost among the Franklin College group was the legendary Robert Toombs (a Demosthenian founder)

front of the problem at the time. The controversy was so widespread that it even aired in the press, frustrating the trustees. Ultimately, however, the trustees (by a narrow vote) backed the president, but at the same time began laying the groundwork for restructuring the University of around a hundred students.

In 1859 Church finally resigned for good (he had earlier resigned in 1857 but was reinstated). The trustees seized the opportunity to install much-needed reforms. They adopted a plan whereby the first- and second-year students would attend an "institute" of the

Lucy Cobb Institute: T.R.R. Cobb raised money for an advanced educational facility for girls in 1858. The institution was named for his daughter, Lucy Cobb, who died of scarlet fever in 1858. Today the building serves as part of the headquarters of the Carl Vinson Institute of Government.

who became secretary of state of the Confederacy. He was a leading candidate for president, but due to his strong and at times overbearing nature, he was passed over for the more moderate Jefferson Davis. He served in the cabinet less than six months before resigning to become a brigadier general in the Confederate Army. His service was highlighted by his Georgia Brigade holding off an entire Union corps at Burnside Bridge for several hours at the Battle of Antietam.

As a young student he was known as a spirited rabble-rouser who was eventually dismissed from the school. Legend has it Toombs came back to the campus and gave such an eloquent speech under a great oak tree that he drew out the commencement audience from the chapel. The truth of the story is question-

able, but nevertheless his legend grows. Tradition has it the oak tree was struck by lightning at the time of Toombs' death. Today a historical marker remains by the stump known as "Toombs' Oak." After the war he fled the country for Cuba and later Europe, barely eluding the Union soldiers who were sent to arrest him. He eventually returned and was, for the rest of his life, a great supporter of the University. Toombs never signed the United States Oath of Allegiance and remained for a lifelong an "unreconstructed rebel."

Of special interest was his lifelong friendship with Alexander H. Stephens. Stephens was elected vice president of the Confederacy. At the University he was known as a "model student," rooming with Crawford W. Long, another "model student." Long had a distin-

Robert Toombs, younger years

Robert Toombs, older years

guished career as a doctor, becoming famous with the discovery of the anesthesia ether. Long and Stephens are the two representatives of Georgia in the National Statuary Hall in the United States Capitol.

Stephens had long opposed secession but bowed to the wishes of the majority in support of the war. However, as the war progressed, he became a constant critic of the policies of Jefferson Davis. He even left Richmond in the middle part of the war and returned to his home, Liberty Hall in Crawfordville. After the war he served the state in the United States Congress and as governor; however, he died in office after serving only six months. He was a University trustee and always championed the cause of his alma mater. He recalled that his "college days were my happiest days." Though not at the college at the same time, he and Toombs later became intimate friends.

This unlikely pair was born only twelve miles apart in Georgia—Toombs in Washington and Stephens in Crawfordville. It was often said they were best of friends (each reserving a special room for the other in their homes), but they never agreed on anything! For sure they disagreed on secession. Toombs was a staunch secessionist, while Stephens argued strongly for the Union. Stephens was joined in the battle to save the Union by Benjamin H. Hill, the first honor graduate of the University in 1844. However, Hill supported Jefferson Davis during the war, and after the war was a longtime supporter of the University. Hill was influential in ending Reconstruction in Georgia while serving in the United States Senate.

The Toombs-Stephens mismatched lifetime relationship was a mystery, considering the opposite personalities and physical stature of the two. Toombs was

Alexander H. Stephens

Benjamin H. Hill

built solid (about six feet four inches tall)—emotional, overbearing, a strong, eloquent speaker with a "healthy thirst for a strong drink." Stephens was about five feet two inches tall, ninety-five pounds, frail (called "Little Aleck"), had a high, shrill voice, and took his "whiskey in spoonfuls" for medicine. They often kidded each other, and Toombs reportedly told Little Aleck during an argument that "I will squash you and eat you up," with Stephens replying, "If you do, you will have more brains in your stomach than you do in your head!"

However, they loved and respected each other. Only Stephens' half-brother, Linton (an 1843 first honor graduate of the college), was closer and more intimate. Linton, who is buried next to his brother at the home place in Crawfordville, became an influential state legislator and member of the Georgia Supreme Court. In the final analysis, Stephens called his friend Toombs a

"genius," a "brilliant lawyer and speaker." But while expressing his love and admiration for him said his true greatness was not 'statesmanship'—he was governed too much by passion and impulse…lacking self-control and mental discipline." Those traits cost him the presidency but served him well in convincing the majority in Georgia to vote for secession. He was joined in this effort by the Cobb brothers of Athens.

Howell Cobb became the first speaker of the provisional government. He had extensive experience in politics serving in the United States Congress (speaker of the house in 1849) and secretary of the treasury in the James Buchanan administration. He chose to serve the Confederacy in the army and obtained the rank of general, spending most of his time in the state heading the home guard. He was a longtime supporter of the University as a trustee.

Howell Cobb

Thomas R. R. Cobb

His younger brother, Thomas R. R. Cobb, blessed with a brilliant legal mind, played a major role in drafting the Constitution of the Confederacy. Cobb, a member of the Board of Trustees, was also an active supporter of the University. He was eventually promoted to brigadier general after forming what became the famous Cobb's legion, and was later killed while leading his men in defense of Marye's Heights at the Battle of Fredericksburg. The historic T.R.R. Cobb House, after experiencing a circuitous route, has been restored and returned to Athens by the Watson-Brown Foundation, Inc. It stands today as a historic house museum under the very capable management of Sam Thomas, a Cobb historian.

The Constitution that was drafted primarily by Cobb is housed in the special collections of The University Library and is unrolled and displayed once a year, on April 26, Confederate Memorial Day. In the future, the library will acquire from me a "very meaningful high plantation style Confederate table" that I secured several years ago. The significance of the table is that it was used by the Confederate Cabinet for the signing of documents, including the Constitution. I acquired the table from a descendent of the family that had originally owned the antique. Through diligent research, I have confirmed the authenticity of the table and its use. The plantation table was presented to the Confederacy in Montgomery to be used for cabinet meetings. The table was given in honor of the marriage of a couple that came from plantations in both south Georgia and south Alabama. The table was owned at the time by a plantation family in Minter, Alabama, just outside Montgomery, called Emerald Place. The master of the plantation, Colonel William Minter, was president of two railroads, representing a strong economic alliance to the Confederacy. The table will eventually be given to the library to join the Constitution upon which the document was signed.

Despite the formation of the Confederate States of America in Montgomery, and later the outbreak of war with the firing on Fort Sumter, Chancellor Lipscomb fought to keep the University open. However, as the fever of war gripped the students and some of the faculty, enrollment plummeted. By 1863, as the fortunes of the war turned against the Confederacy, coupled with the pending threat that Georgia might be invaded, the chancellor and the trustees were forced to make the decision to close the University in October of that year. It is estimated that during the course of the war, several hundred students, faculty, and alumni entered the war, and some 100 paid the ultimate sacrifice.

Fighting for Their Cause

The first prominent university graduate to give his life in defense of the southern cause was Francis R. Bartow, a fervent secessionist from Savannah. In fact, Bartow became the first brigade commander to be killed in the Civil War. He became a hero after being killed leading his regiments to victory in the first Battle of Bull Run.

A lesser-known University casualty, but one of my favorite Confederate officers, was William Delony who graduated first in the class of 1846 and practiced law in Athens. After the war started, he raised a cavalry company known as the Georgia Troopers and was elected captain of Company C of Cobb's Legion Cavalry Battalion. He was a game and aggressive fighter, participating in numerous engagements and receiving several serious wounds. He became a hero in the retreat from Gettysburg when the long wagon train of the wounded was about to be overrun by the Union Cavalry at

Francis R. Bartow

Charlestown, West Virginia, just prior to crossing the Potomac. Delony, who earlier was promoted to lieutenant colonel, had received a saber wound to his head but rallied some 200 wounded Confederates still capable of fighting and formed a perimeter that helped to beat back the Union Cavalry. He was later wounded, captured, and died in a federal hospital in Washington. He was buried there, then brought home to be reinterred in the Oconee Hill Cemetery in his hometown. He was a devoted husband and father, and the University library has stacks of letters written during the war between him and his beloved wife, Rosa.

Better known was Henry L. Benning, an honor graduate in 1834 at the University of Georgia, who rose to the rank of general while leading a Georgia regiment in combat. He took part in many engagements

John B. Gordon

a superb officer who suffered five gunshot wounds at Antietam and miraculously survived. Toward the end of the war he was promoted to a corps commander in Lee's Army and was accorded the honor of heading the Confederate Army in the official surrender at Appomattox. He was elected three times to the United States Senate and was also elected governor of the state. He is buried in Atlanta in Oakland Cemetery and is memorialized on the grounds of the State Capitol with an equestrian statue that portrays the general astride his horse, Marye.

The University did produce one prominent Union soldier during the Civil War, Stephen Vincent Benet. He attended Georgia in 1844 before transferring to West Point. Benet remained in the regular army after the war, rising to the rank of general and becoming chief of ordnance of the United States Army. Of special note is the fact that his grandson, the famous American poet Stephen Vincent Benet, came to the University and presented a portrait of his grandfather to the school where it remains in the Georgia Museum of Art. The younger Benet was best known for his epic poem of the Civil War, *John Brown's Body*, which earned him the Pulitzer Prize in 1929.

The War Comes to the University

The University campus became the site of Civil War activity both during and after the war. In August 1864, a Union Cavalry Corps under General George Stoneman (historically identified as Stoneman's Raid) was defeated near Clinton, Georgia, at the Battle of Sunshine Church. Stoneman and some 900 men of his cavalry corp surrendered. Two Union brigades were able to escape and headed to Athens to destroy the Confederate Cook Brothers Armory. Thwarted by the Athens home guard, one brigade, under Colonel Horace Capron, headed to Winder, Georgia, where they were defeated by the Confederate Cavalry at the Battle of Jugs Tavern near the Mulberry River.

Some 200 Union soldiers (and an additional 200 more over the next few days) and a like number of horses and mules were marched into Athens and deposited behind the wrought-iron fence surrounding the University, where they were held prisoner for two

from Second Manassas to Appomattox Courthouse and was severely wounded at the Wilderness. He was called "Old Rock," and his nickname testified to his soldierly qualities. He survived the war and returned to his hometown of Columbus to resume his law practice. Fort Benning, the officers training school in Columbus, was named in his honor.

Perhaps the most famous of the Confederate soldiers who attended the University of Georgia, though he dropped out after a couple of years in 1852, was General John B. Gordon. He is credited for having "one of the most spectacular wartime and post-bellum careers of any civilian who fought for the Confederacy." He was

Former UGA students who fought for the Confederacy in the Civil War

days. They were then shipped by train to Andersonville Prison Stockade. During their stay, Colonel William B. Breckinridge and his 9th Kentucky Cavalry, who had captured the Union Cavalry were given a hero's welcome at the college chapel by the University and the city. A rabid Bulldog fan once asked me if they had rung the chapel bell during the celebration of victory over the Union Cavalry as a precursor to the ringing of chapel bell after football victories. After a good laugh, I was able to research and find that in the 1890s the

chapel was located next to Herty Field, and the frosh were required to ring the bell until midnight celebrating a Bulldog victory. When I was coaching, my wife, Barbara, always took our children to ring the chapel bell after a victory.

After the war Union troops occupied the city and several of the University buildings. While Chancellor Lipscomb did his best to cooperate with the occupying forces, there is little doubt that Athenians and college personnel at the time resented the presence of the

The Civil War–era double-barrel cannon, now at City Hall in Athens, never worked as intended. Two cannon balls chained together were to be fired simultaneously, but the timing was always off, and the two cannon balls went careening out of control.

Yankee soldiers. The resentment built up by the town and gown over the occupying forces was exacerbated when it was reported that Phi Kappa Hall, occupied by the Federals, had "been badly defaced" and that Union "rifle practice had taken place with the columns of the chapel as the targets." Lipscomb was able to eventually persuade the occupying commanders to remove the troops from the campus. Despite the conciliatory efforts of Chancellor Lipscomb, the tension remained on campus throughout the Reconstruction period.

One positive in the post-war era was the acquisition in 1868 of artist George Cook's painting of the *Interior of St. Peter's Cathedral in Rome* (circa 1847). Cook's patron, Daniel Pratt, an Alabama industrialist who once lived in Milledgeville, presented the huge oil painting on canvas to the University, and it was soon hung in the chapel. At the time it was the largest framed oil painting in the world, and today, some 140 years later, it still hangs in the chapel. Another Cook painting of interest to the University is his *View of Athens from Carr's Hill* (1845) that is housed in the Hargrett

Rare Book and Manuscript Library. The scene depicting antebellum Athens and the University from Carr's Hill, where the railroad tracks ended, is found in most Athens/University history books. The Cook paintings were a brief respite from a multitude of post-war problems on campus.

A Short-Lived Progressive University

After the war the University, like the rest of the South, was on the verge of financial disaster. The school was near bankruptcy. However, thanks to the Morrill Act, the college was able to survive. The Morrill Act was passed by the United States Congress during the war to promote for "practical value" nationwide agriculture and mechanical land grant colleges. It eventually became a godsend to the University. Federal funds from the legislation enabled the College of Agriculture and Mechanical Arts to open in 1872. In the same year, the Medical College of Georgia in Augusta became part of the University. These additions delighted Chancel-

Sketch of George Cook's *Interior of St. Peter's Cathedral in Rome*

lor Lipscomb. He was long committed to modernizing the University by emphasizing public service to help the state develop both economically and socially.

The optimism didn't last long. Chancellor Lipscomb's dream of a progressive university essentially died when he retired in 1873. The next three chancellors (Henry H. Tucker 1874-78, Patrick H. Mell 1878-88, and William E. Boggs 1889-99) reverted to a more conservative philosophy, perhaps in conformity with the state still trying to recover from the war. The University once again essen-

tially became a traditional liberal arts college.

During these post-war years prior to the turn of the century, the University remained stagnant. It received, as in the past, little funding from the state. Meanwhile, as the century turned, the population of the state rose to almost 2 million. The University enrollment, however, was less than 300. Thus the all-male, all-white school continued on the path of serving an elite minority of the state population.

College Avenue and Broad Street in the early 1920s

INTO THE TWENTIETH CENTURY

Henry W. Grady

One elite student who later represented a point of pride for the University was Henry W. Grady, the son of a wealthy plantation owner in Athens. He was reared by his mother after his soldier/father was killed at Petersburg in 1864. While he was a student at the University, from 1865-68, he lived in what is now called the Taylor-Grady House. The Southern mansion has been restored and today is one of the grand plantation homes utilized for social events in the Classic City. Grady became famous as a journalist (editor of *The Atlanta Constitution*) and as an orator promoting the "New South" philosophy of national unification, diversified farming, southern industrial growth, and northern investments. While he has had his critics over the years, especially regarding his "moderate" views on equal rights, he was a "national hero," and his fame provided much-needed prestige and credibility to the University's journalism school. The school was founded in 1921 and is named in his honor.

Thanks to the leadership of some excellent deans such as the legendary John E. Drewry, the journalism school reputation has grown immensely.

Henry W. Grady

It was Dean Drewry who maximized the generosity of George Foster Peabody, a Columbus, Georgia native who moved to New York and made millions in the banking business. Peabody became a great benefactor to the school, and Dean Drewry directed that generosity into the George Foster Peabody Awards that are recognized today as the "Pulitzer Prize of radio and television." Dean Drewry retired in 1969, and in 1988 the school was elevated to college status and is now the Henry W. Grady College of Journalism and Mass Communication. If alive, Drewry, I am sure, would be the first (though there are many) to point to "Lessie" Bailey Smithgall, a former Georgia student, as the one initially responsible for the Peabody Awards being at the University. Lessie, who was working at WSB at the time, introduced Dean Drewry to Lambdin Kay, general manager of the station, and their efforts led to the establishment of the George Foster Peabody Awards at the University. I was privileged to attend Lessie's 100th birthday party in

Gainesville in April of 2011. This amazing woman has been a marvelous supporter of the University, though her late husband, Charles, was a great supporter of Georgia Tech. The Smithgalls endowed the Lambdin Kay Chair that is occupied by the current director of the Peabody Awards, Horace Newcomb.

Dr. Charles H. Herty: A True Renaissance Man

Despite the many problems of the post-war period, some good news appeared as the century turned. The University managed to employ a new generation of professors, primarily from Virginia, who for the most part proved to be competent and long tenured. Interestingly, one of the most gifted of those professors who made the greatest, long-term impact was Charles H. Herty, a non-Virginian who had a short tenure at the University.

Charles Herty, from Milledgeville, Georgia, described as "a true Renaissance man," was an 1886 first honor graduate of the University, studying chemistry and earning a bachelor of philosophy degree. He received his PhD in chemistry from Johns Hopkins and returned to the University to teach. After eight years with no promotion or salary raise, he left the school for the University of North Carolina, where he became chair of the chemistry department and later dean of the School of Applied Science.

All the while, he was a strong national advocate of chemistry, and he eventually resigned from the university at Chapel Hill to become full-time editor of the journal of the American Chemical Society. He then embarked on a mission of speaking the gospel of chemistry across the country to business and government leaders, and became known nationally as "the mouthpiece for chemistry."

Herty became famous internationally when in 1903 he developed a simple method to collect pine resin without scarring or damaging the trees. He formed the Herty Turpentine Cup Industry in Savannah to manufacture the collection apparatus. This simple device, used for almost a century, saved the southern pine forests and the United States turpentine and resin industry from extinction.

During the Great Depression of the 1930s he was

Candler Hall opened in 1902 as a dormitory. It is named for Governor Allen Daniel Candler.

driven to help the southern economy that had hit rock bottom. The crisis led him to develop the idea of using cheap and fast-growing southern pines as a resource to make newsprint and white paper. His work created an untold number of jobs and had a stunning positive impact on the southern economy. For those works and many more, he has been labeled as "the most important American-born twentieth-century U.S. chemist." His many contributions are kept alive by the Herty Medal, an award given annually by the American Chemical Society to worthy recipients promoting the industry.

Despite his amazing accomplishments national-ly and internationally, he is most remembered by the greatest majority of those who follow the University as the "father of Georgia football." Herty was always interested in sports. He played baseball, and while in school he vividly recalled some of his first impressions of the crudeness of athletics at the University. When he returned from Johns Hopkins he immediately brought to life campus athletics while serving as the first faculty athletic director. He raised money for facilities, built tennis courts, and constructed the first campus gymna-sium in the basement of the Old College. He organized intercollegiate baseball, coaching the first varsity team

1898 football team

while playing centerfield. It was during those times around 1890 that red and black became the official school colors. Prior to that, the colors were red, black, and gold, but the petition to the trustees to eliminate yellow because they did "not want any yellow in Georgia athletics" moved the trustees to officially adopt red and black.

But it was the new game of football that fascinated Herty. He learned of the game at Johns Hopkins with classmate George Petrie of Auburn, who was working on his PhD in history. Both were captured by the game and vowed that when they returned to their respective campuses they would each start a football team and play each other. At that time no collegiate game of football had ever been played south of Raleigh, North Carolina.

Herty taught the game to students while carrying a Walter Camp rulebook he had acquired in Baltimore. The players helped their coach prepare a "gridiron" on the old playing field. That field later became known as Herty Field, where all outdoor athletic events took place until 1911. The field later became a parking lot, and I vividly recall dedicating a historical marker in the fall of 1991 during the celebration of the 100th anniversary of football at Georgia. The plaque commemorates Herty Field, where the first Georgia football game was played and the first intercollegiate game in the Deep South was also played. Representing the Herty family at the dedication was the nephew of the late Dr. Herty, Charles Herty Hooper who was the University of Georgia's oldest tennis letterman. Today, the area is a beautiful green space accompanied by a gorgeous fountain.

The first game was played against Mercer on January 30, 1892. (As an aside, the first Georgia team average height was five feet eight, and the average weight was 156 pounds. The 2011 team's average is about six feet three and the weight is 260! This makes the modern team five inches taller and 104 pounds heavier!) In those earlier days the game, according to Athens historian the late Dr. John Stegeman, son of coach and athletic director Herman J. Stegeman, was a "cruel and grueling push-and-pull affair" not conducive to scoring. However, Georgia surprisingly rolled over the Macon school 50-0! After the game "enthusiasm was supreme" read the local paper, *The Banner.* "When the game ended," the paper reported, "the boys were riding

around on a sea of shoulders. Even the goat, Georgia's first mascot was ridden."

It was further reported at the time that Georgia was "hooked for good, and the excitement exploded in anticipation of the next game against Auburn." The 50-0 trouncing of Mercer might have made the Georgia team and their followers a little overconfident as they began preparation for their second game against the boys from the "loveliest village of the plain."

Doctors Herty and Petrie agreed to play the game on a neutral site in Atlanta's Piedmont Park on February 20, 1892. The city of Atlanta was full of excitement that day with "brass bands playing and the colors of both schools flying all over the city." Both teams arrived by train along with their entourage sporting the respective school colors. Georgia's mascot, the goat, was decked out in red and black.

However, it was not a good day for the boys of Athens, as they were shut out by Auburn, 10-0. The Georgia contingent was in total shock. It was reported (though unconfirmed) that the Georgia students and fans were so depressed that they barbecued the goat, ending forever the career of Georgia's first mascot. It also marked the end of the two-game career of Georgia's first coach, Charles Herty, who turned his attention to his life work in chemistry.

While the mascot and the coach of Georgia ended their careers after only one year, it was just the beginning of the longest football series in the Deep South between those two great rivals of neighboring states. As of this writing, since 1892 the two teams have played a total of 114 games, and only two games separate the records of the teams. Auburn has won 54 games and Georgia 52 with 8 ties in the grand and ancient rivalry.

I was directly involved in this great rivalry for some fifty-two years, having the unique experience of seeing the action from both sidelines. I played and then coached at Auburn for a total of twelve years and coached and/or served as athletic director at Georgia for forty years. There are a lot of similarities in these two great institutions, and the rivalry is appropriately between "feudin' cousins."

Following Dr. Herty, Georgia had some renowned coaches and players during those early days on the southern gridiron. Hall of Famer Glenn S. "Pop" Warner coached for two years and had an undefeated team

First played at UGA in 1886, baseball was the earliest sport at the University.

Richard Von Gammon and plaque in his memory

in 1896 before embarking on a stellar coaching career up north. Alex Cunningham was an outstanding coach from 1910-1919. He was blessed to have Georgia's first All-American and Hall of Famer, Bob McWhorter, who later became a professor in the law school and mayor of Athens.

During those early years, a crisis arose that might have eliminated the sport, at least for an indefinite period of time.

The Von Gammon Tragedy

In 1897, Richard Von Gammon, of Rome, Georgia, received a serious head injury in a game against Virginia, (no helmets were worn in those early years) that eventually led to his death. The entire state was in shock as Georgia, Georgia Tech, and Mercer all immediate-ly disbanded football. The Georgia General Assembly responded by passing a bill outlawing the game in Georgia. *The Atlanta Journal* responded with a head-line that read "Death Knell of Football." However, Von Gammon's mother wrote a letter that was given to the governor asking that "my boy's death...not be used to defeat the most cherished object of his life." The gover-nor was so moved by the mother's appeal, he refused to sign the bill, thereby saving the game in the state.

Georgia and Virginia met again in Athens in 1921, and the officials of "Mr. Jefferson's University" presented a beautiful bronze plaque to the University in memory of Richard Von Gammon. The plaque depicts a sorrow-ful mother looking down holding her limp son at her feet while he sadly gazes up at her. The inscription at the top of the plaque reads "A mother's strength pre-vailed." The plaque hangs today in the Butts-Mehre Heritage Hall. Many a visitor has paused to admire the beautiful plaque and the inspiring story of a mother's love and strength that saved the game of football in Georgia.

The First National Championship

During the 1920s Georgia had two outstanding foot-ball coaches, Herman J. Stegeman and George "Kid" Woodruff. Stegeman coached for three years with his first team going undefeated (8-0-1) in 1920. Stegeman coached all the Georgia major sports and was dean of men and the faculty chair from 1920 to 1936. One of his star track pupils was none other than distance runner William Tate, who later succeeded Stegeman as dean of men. Named in his memory is Stegeman Coliseum, which is home for Georgia basketball and gymnastics and graduation exercises during inclement weather.

George "Kid" Woodruff of Columbus, Georgia, was one of the University's most devoted alumni. He agreed to coach the football team for a dollar a year during some financially difficult times. He was Georgia's coach from 1923 to 1927, leading his last team to a 9-1 re-cord and a National Championship in two polls. The 1927 team, known as "the dream and wonder team," produced two All-Americans, I.M. Chuck Shiver Jr. of Sylvester, Georgia, and Tom A. Nash of Washington, Georgia. Nash played professionally for five years for

Cadet Corps drills

Green Bay, including three championships in 1929, '30 and '32. His son was an All-SEC tackle for me on our 1971 (11-1) team and became a highly respected lawyer in Savannah. Woodruff retired after the 1927 season but remained an active supporter of athletics and the University. He passed the torch to Harry Mehre, who had been an assistant on the staff. Woodruff had earlier hired him upon the recommendation of the immortal Knute Rockne to install the "Notre Dame system."

Winning the national championship in 1927, brought attention to Georgia throughout the country. Mehre brought further national attention to Georgia during his reign as coach by beating the Yale Bulldogs, a national powerhouse, five straight times. The success of the football team attracted many fans and supporters who had never attended the University, and they increasingly became the catalysts that literally spread the University throughout the entire state.

A State University

Under the strong leadership of two of the University's most progressive chancellors, the next quarter century saw the school emerge as a major state university. Walter B. Hill served as chancellor from 1899 until his death in 1905 and was succeeded almost immediately by David C. Barrow, the dean of Franklin College of Arts and Sciences, who served nineteen years, from 1906 to 1925. Barrow, affectionately called "Uncle Dave," was so well loved and respected that in the middle of his long tenure as president, the Georgia General Assembly in 1914 named a newly formed county (with Winder as the seat) in his honor. Both men shared a lot in common and a similar philosophy of what a modern university should be. Hill and Barrow became the first two University graduates and the first two non-clergy to lead the University in one hundred years. Both exhibited excellent public relations skills, cultivating for the first time good relationships with the state legislature and philanthropic supporters. Both believed strongly that the school should provide "public service" for the people of the state of Georgia.

No one carried out the definition of a "state university" more than Andrew M. Soule, president of the newly restructured College of Agriculture and Mechanical Arts in 1906. He ruled the Agriculture and Mechanical Arts College for some twenty-five years, constantly touring the state (often irritating people along the way) proclaiming that his operation was, as University historian F. N. Boney wrote, "The College with the state for its campus."

In rapid succession, individual schools and colleges were created across an expanded campus under chancellors Hill and Barrow. The pharmacy school was instituted in 1903 followed by the School of Forestry in 1906. The school of education started in 1908 and the graduate school in 1910. The school of commerce began in 1912, followed by journalism in 1915.

Many buildings were constructed during those first two decades to house the newly formed schools on campus. Foremost was Agriculture Hall completed in 1909 (renamed Connor Hall) atop "Ag Hill" on the newly opened twenty-five-acre South Campus. By 1928 the South Campus had grown to over 200 acres with many new buildings. Student enrollment accelerated as the campus expanded, growing from fewer than 300 at the turn of the century to more than 1,600 by 1925.

World War I

Student military training was commonplace at the University in the late nineteenth century. Drills held by the Cadet Corps on Herty Field were accelerated with the outbreak of World War I. It is estimated that some one thousand men from the University served in the war, with forty-seven paying the ultimate price for their country.

The most noted casualty was Henry Lee J. Williams who was valedictorian of the class of 1907, a Rhodes Scholar and captain of the Cadet Corps. He married Chancellor Barrow's daughter and was later killed in France while serving as an Episcopalian chaplain. Wil-

liams was honored several years ago by the famed 82nd Airborne Division as the first man from the division to fall in World War I. All of those killed in action in the war were honored in 1925 with the dedication of the student activities building—called Memorial Hall. The building, located next to Sanford Stadium, has been used by the University in various ways for some ninety years. It was financed by the most ambitious fundraising effort to that point in the University's history. Through the leadership of University graduate (1893) Harry Hodgson, an Athens businessman, the fund drive netted over $1 million.

A Co-educational University

The most significant reform during the Progressive Era of the early twentieth century came in 1918 when the University admitted women for the first time as regular students. Earlier the school had allowed women to attend summer school for teachers but this decision was not relatively forward looking at the time. In fact, compared to other schools in the Southeast, Georgia was among the last schools to admit women.

Agriculture School President Andrew Soule, seeing the need for women in nutrition and extension work, became the prime supporter of the admission of women to the University. In recognition of his progressive leadership, the first women's dorm, completed in 1920, was named in his honor.

Mary Creswell, the first woman to receive an undergraduate degree at the school, became department head of home economics under Soule's agriculture college. Earlier, Mary Lyndon, who received a master's degree in 1914, was named dean of women. She was succeeded by Anne W. Brumby, who carried on the work of integrating women to campus life. Brumby, Creswell, and Lyndon are familiar buildings dedicated to the memories of those pioneer women who led the admission of women at the University.

Georgia vs. Georgia Tech Rivalry

The rivalry between Georgia and Georgia Tech became so bitter prior to World War I that the two institutions discontinued playing each other for five years, from

Mary Creswell

1919 through 1924. While heated athletic competition between the two institutions was the visible sign of the conflict, there had been an undercurrent of resentment between the two schools for some time.

Shortly after the turn of the century, there were seven public institutions of higher education in the state, including Georgia Tech. Technically, each of the institutions operated as branches of the University of Georgia. As the institutions became more independent, this arrangement grew increasingly irritating. This was particularly true of Georgia Tech, which had its own board of trustees.

Over the years leading up to World War I, Tech had become a well-respected institution, and its ties with the growing community of Atlanta enabled it to flex its independence. The tensions between Tech and Georgia worsened as the schools became competitive in pursuit of state and federal funding. This was particularly true when "Tech made a progressive attempt to win a portion of the land grant funds." University historian Thomas G. Dyer wrote that Tech's proposed legislation to take half of the funds so infuriated Georgia partisans that "open warfare very nearly erupted with the University." These underlying irritations between the two schools became more public and expressive as baseball and football competition stirred the emotions and passion of alumni and supporters.

The Georgia-Georgia Tech rivalry heated up after the first game played in 1893. Tech won 28-6, led by a running back who scored three touchdowns. Running around, between and over the Georgia players, he looked like a man playing against boys. Turned out, he was! The man was thirty-three-year-old army surgeon Captain Leonard Wood, who was stationed at Fort McPherson and asked to coach the Tech team. Not content with coaching, Wood put himself in the game and became an unadulterated "ringer" in the lineup against Georgia. The Georgia fans did not know who Wood was until the next day when *The Atlanta Journal* reported "the University of Georgia was defeated...not by a Technological school...but a United States Army surgeon." Dr. Wood had earlier served at the Arizona-Mexico border, where he won the Congressional Medal of Honor for fighting Apaches and being largely responsible for capturing Geronimo. The Georgia fans were incensed with this dastardly fraudulent act by Tech to win the game.

The rivalry really heated up during a two-game baseball series in Atlanta in 1919 that was won by Georgia. In the first game, the Tech brass band left the grandstand at a critical moment late in the game, gathered near the base paths, and "blared forth" harassing the Georgia pitcher. Georgia still won, but after the game fights broke out in the streets of Atlanta between several Georgia and Tech fans.

The following weekend in Athens, during the traditional senior parade, the Georgia students designed a replica of a World War I tank, followed immediately in the parade by a Model-T Ford driven by two Georgia students.

The tank banner read—GEORGIA IN FRANCE

Looking toward downtown Athens from inside the iron fence

1917-1918 (Georgia disbanded football during those two years of the war.)

The Model-T banner read—TECH IN ATLANTA 1917-1918 (Tech continued to play football in those years.)

The implications that the Georgia boys were serving their country in war in France while the Tech boys were home so infuriated the Tech people they broke off athletic relations. The two schools did not play for five years. Finally, in 1925 Governor Clifford Walker called the Georgia and Tech presidents to his office essentially ordering them to renew the series.

Governor Walker's son, Harold Walker, a fourth-generation Georgia graduate, was the longtime "poet laureate" of the Georgia Bulldogs. Harold Walker, who later served on the UGA Athletic Board, also wrote many inspiring poems about the team especially during my early years as head coach. However, his most famous poem might well have been "The Man Who Broke the Drought," memorializing fullback Theron Sapp. His one-yard run against Georgia Tech in 1957 broke an eight-game losing streak to the "eternal enemy." The phrase "eternal enemy" was coined by Georgia's legend and ultra successful Hartman, are the greatest Bulldogs who ever lived. Magill was the sports information director (SID) for many years and coined a lot of Bulldog phrases. He was a good friend of the "poet laureate" and compiled a booklet of Walker's inspiring poems titled *Bulldoggerel.*

Speaking of the Bulldogs, many connect the Geor-

Uga at the Chapel Bell

gia mascot to the early strong ties the University had with Yale, whose mascot was a Bulldog. This is a logical theory but not true. Research has found that the nickname "Bulldog" was used sporadically for baseball and football during the 1910s by Atlanta newspaper writers. However, the Bulldog mascot was used consistently about midway into the 1920 football season. Morgan Blake, of *The Atlanta Journal*, wrote that the nickname bulldog would sound good because "there is a certain dignity about a bulldog as well as ferocity." That same year, Cliff Wheatley of *The Atlanta Constitution* used the name "bulldog" in his story five times, and the name has stuck ever since.

During the first half century there were several different Bulldog mascots with a variety of names. Georgia's greatest era of Bulldog mascots started in 1956 with Frank "Sonny" Seiler, a "double Dawg" graduate (undergraduate 1956 and law school 1957) from Savannah. He introduced a white English bulldog named Uga I to the "Dawg" nation. Since that time, there have been seven Uga descendants of Uga I, all cared for by Seiler, his wife Cecelia and the Seiler family. All of the Ugas have attained celebrity status among the Georgia faithful, and some have even reached national renown. Uga V appeared on the cover of *Sports Illustrated* in 1997 and was acclaimed the number one mascot in the nation. He also played his father, Uga IV, in the film by Clint Eastwood "Midnight in the Garden of Good and Evil." Unfortunately in recent years, to the distress of the Seiler family and the Bulldog nation, health problems saw the early demise of Uga VII (four-year reign) and Uga VIII (four-month reign), which has caused a direct descendant problem. As of this writing, "Russ" is currently filling in as a substitute similar to "Otto." Otto served the remainder of the 1986 season after Uga III tore a ligament in his leg leaping off the bed the morning before the Vanderbilt game.

Other Georgia traditions also began in the 1900s. In the mid-twenties, Hugh Hodgson of the class of 1915 wrote the words "Glory, Glory to Old Georgia" to the tune of the "Battle Hymn of the Republic," despite its being one of the Union Army's favorite songs during the Civil War. Ironically, the same thing happened at Auburn. When I was in school the fight song was "Glory, Glory to Old Auburn." I am happy that in the late 1950s, Mr. Roy Sewell, an Auburn enthusiast and clothing manufacturer from Bremen, Georgia, financed the writing of a new fight song that turned out to be "War Eagle." This in turn provided exclusive fight song rights to "Glory, Glory to old Georgia." Meanwhile, "Dixie" was always played during the game arousing the spirit of the Bulldog faithful. This came to an end (for good and bad) in the mid 1970s when the Dixie Redcoat Band dropped the name Dixie and quit playing the inspiring but controversial tune.

When Georgia and Tech resumed playing each other in football in 1925, the games were played on Grant Field, because Tech's stadium seated more than 20,000 fans, twice as many as Georgia's old Sanford Field. Tech won all four of those games, and when they upset the undefeated Georgia team of 1927, knocking them out of the Rose Bowl, the fans were humiliated and infuriated. Thus entered Steadman V. Sanford, one of the University's most effective servants.

Steadman Vincent Sanford

No one has served the University of Georgia in a more diverse way for a longer period of time than Steadman V. Sanford. He arrived in 1903 as an English professor, after serving several years as teacher, principal, and superintendent of secondary schools in Marietta. He also taught journalism at the University and in 1921 founded the Henry W. Grady School of Journalism.

During the early years he became faculty chairman of athletics (1907) and helped sponsor the campus newspaper *The Red and Black*, which became the official organ for athletics. He was instrumental in founding the Southern Athletic Conference (forerunner of the Southeastern Conference) and was appointed its first president.

In those early years the king of sports was baseball, and Sanford wanted a better facility than old Herty Field. He was responsible for picking the site, soliciting support, and dedicating what became known as Sanford Field in 1911. The grandstand was constructed for baseball, but the complex was used for football as well. The site, in front of the current Sanford Stadium, was also for many years the location of Stegeman Hall, home of Georgia's physical education and athletic offices (my first office in 1964) and the historic old swim-

Steadman V. Sanford

---

ming pool. Built for the navy in 1943, it became ancient and a recruiting liability in the 1970s and '80s while other schools were building modern complexes. Before Georgia built a modern facility, ultra successful swimming coach Jack Bauerle sold old Stegeman Pool as the country's "fastest swimming pool," affording great opportunity for record setting. Today the area is a parking lot in front of the Tate Student Activities building and Sanford Stadium.

Sanford also dedicated Woodruff Hall in 1923. At the time it was a modern 3,000-seat multipurpose arena (but was used primarily for basketball), which is now the location of the psychology-journalism complex. While at Auburn, I played basketball in what had become "ancient" Woodruff Hall against Georgia in the early 1950s. The facility was for many years an asset to Georgia basketball coach Harbin "Red" Lawson, who kept his job despite thirteen straight losing seasons. Combining good humor and public relations skills, Lawson always joked that both "the wind and the rain were strategic factors in the old arena." Lawson's coaching career came to an end shortly after modern

Stegeman Coliseum was inaugurated in 1964.

For all of Professor Sanford's accomplishments at the University, both athletically and academically, it was the building of Sanford Stadium that he is best known for. His dream of a stadium on the college campus was formulated after the disastrous fourth straight loss to Tech in 1927 that knocked Georgia out of the Rose Bowl.

The site selected by Sanford in the valley of Tanyard Creek, which separates North and South campus, was a no-brainer in retrospect. It proved to be a beautiful site and economically sound with the grandstands resting against each side of the valley and requiring little structural support. A concrete culvert some seven feet high by ten feet wide was built to accommodate the creek flowing under the field.

The total cost of the stadium is estimated between $300,000 and $360,000. Financing turned out to be relatively easy after a mechanism was set up to borrow money not legally feasible for the University. In 1929, the Athletic Association was incorporated, which was essential in securing a loan. The decision did receive some criticism for fear the action took athletics from under the authority of the administration.

This was especially true after the charter was renewed in 1949. While the arrangement was financially necessary, it did raise some problems that needed addressing. As one who was directly involved with the situation for some forty years, there were challenges and some justifiable criticism. However, with the incorporation of most all of the administrative structure through the University, most of the problems have been resolved. The very capable vice president for business and finance of the University, Dr. Allan W. Barber (1971–2000), was primarily responsible for setting up a close and efficient financial working relationship with the association, which included bringing retirement under the University umbrella. At the same time, the separate corporation provides the benefits of borrowing and creative financing not possible through the University. By law the separate corporation assures the University and the people of the state that no public funds will ever be used for athletics. This mandate has the effect of challenging the Athletic Association to run an $80 million to $90 million budget and employ a sound business enterprise all within the framework of a university business structure.

UGA's first baseball field, old Herty Field

All large projects ultimately must have the approval of the Georgia Board of Regents, which becomes the ultimate beneficiary. As an example, every athletic facility that has been built and paid for by the association (over $190 million) is turned over to the Board of Regents in perpetuity. Meanwhile, 85-plus percent of the athletic budget that funds all the sport programs comes from football revenue. There are only two athletic teams, football and men's basketball, that generate a profit, thereby funding all twenty-one men and women sports that are sponsored by the University of Georgia Athletic Association.

Sanford was often criticized for his emphasis on intercollegiate athletics, and especially football, but he never hesitated to defend the value of sports at the University. As dean of the University he reported on the 1927-28 school year: "The main indictment against intercollegiate athletics, particularly football, is overemphasis. Certainly there is an overemphasis, but not nearly so much by college students and college faculties as by the American people."

Nevertheless, thanks to the Association's incorporation in 1929, and the leadership of Sanford, approximately $180,000 was borrowed from an Atlanta bank against the guarantee of some "guarantors." Two hundred and twenty-seven loyal supporters and alumni pledged either $500 or $1,000 to ensure the stadium loan against default. The loan was paid off with no problem, and those loyal supporters were rewarded with fifty-yard-line seats for life. I remember in the early 1980s the last living guarantor, Mercer Sherman, who was living in Albany, Georgia, died. The names of all those faithful alumni and supporters are inscribed over a picture of the original stadium with the title *Friends and Alumni of Georgia Who Made the Stadium Possible*. The stadium and guarantors' picture appeared in the issue of the October 1929 Georgia Alumni Record.

Sanford was able to garner support for the stadium from both local and state governments. The Athens-Clarke County workforce and convict labor (the custom in those days) were responsible for clearing the site prior to building the stadium. When completed in 1929, the stadium could seat 33,000. As of 2011 it seats almost 93,000 with seventy-seven luxury sky suites.

Sanford wanted to dedicate the stadium with a grand celebration. He was able to persuade the Yale administration to bring the great Yale team south to participate in the dedication. This marked the first time in history that Yale had left its "New England home… to travel south." It was a natural matchup between the two schools that shared so much in common. Yale's coming to Athens was a coup for Georgia, representing the institution's "greatest rise to national prominence." There was never any question as to what the stadium would be named. It was called Sanford Stadium, as it is today almost ninety years later.

The game and the events surrounding the classic are legendary. Yale came by train, and at every stop, crowds gathered to gawk at the mighty Yale team. After the team arrived, the Yale "boola boola" band paraded down the streets of Athens, and to the delight of many southerners who were seeing "Yankees" for the first time, the band struck up "Hail to Georgia Down in Dixie." *The Atlanta Georgian* newspaper covered the arrival and the anticipated event with pictures and bold headlines on the front page.

Thanks to some old film that was salvaged and converted to video, I have been able to see a portion of the dedication and the game. The DVD starts with the Yale band marching on the field followed by the Yale team. Next came the Georgia band followed by the Georgia team. The ceremony begins but the film is cut short and fuzzy. I was later told by the 1929 Yale block-ing back Robert Hall, whom I had met many years ago in New York at the Hall of Fame, that the "ceremony lasted an hour and we were in our wool uniforms. We melted in that Georgia heat and humidity." Hall said the Yale team was "finished when the game started." By dominating the game from the opening kickoff, Georgia made sure that Yale was finished, as the Bulldogs of Athens shutout the Bulldogs of New Haven, 15-0. All-American and Hall of Famer Vernon "Catfish" Smith scored all the points. The DVD has most all of the football action, highlighted by tailback Spurgeon Chandler (later New York Yankee pitching great) throwing a sixty-yard touchdown pass to "Catfish" Smith. It was a glorious day and the culmination of Sanford's many contributions to the University through athletics. Most all of his attention was now turned to administrating the University and eventually the state system.

U.S. Senator Richard B. Russell and University President S.V. Sanford

While athletics had dominated Sanford's life up to this time, the rest of his life was devoted to his career as an educator. Even while he was putting all of his energy into building the stadium and preparing for the dedication, he was acting as president of the Franklin College and dean of the University. He was appointed to the position in 1926 when Charles M. Snelling was appointed chancellor. Snelling was chancellor of the University for only six years but toward the end of his administration (1930 and 1931) he served during one of the most significant developments in the history of higher education in Georgia. This development had its roots in the severe economic condition the state was experiencing during the Great Depression.

Richard B. Russell, a 1918 (LLB) Georgia graduate from Winder, campaigned for governor in 1930 on a platform for better efficiency in state government. Following his election, a part of fulfilling his campaign promise was to reorganize higher education under a consolidated board of regents. This structure was a dramatic change eliminating the many higher education boards of trustees of various public institutions in the state.

View of old campus from Broad Street

Since its nineteenth-century construction, the downtown building that is now the Georgia Theatre has served as a YMCA, a hotel, a Masonic Temple, a worship hall, and a concert venue popular with students. It was renovated in 2011 and reopened after a major fire.

Leading the change for the board of regents educational reform were two University graduates, Hughes Spalding, who received his law degree in 1910, and Phillip Weltner, who received his undergraduate degree in 1907. Spalding chaired the new consolidated board, and as a friend and supporter of Steadman Sanford, helped him to resolve the growing conflict with the controversial State College of Agriculture president, Andrew M. Soule.

On January 1, 1932, the Board of Regents named Snelling head of the entire university system with the new title of chancellor. At the same time, they restored the position of president as head of the University (gone since 1859) and elevated Sanford to the position. It was in his new position as president that Sanford came in direct conflict with the controlling Soule, who had for years been pushing for an Agriculture College completely independent of the University. Sanford on the other hand was in favor of consolidating all units as part of the school. It was the strong leadership of Spalding and Weltner that won the day for Sanford. Spalding chaired the regents in the spring of 1932 when they voted to combine the Agriculture College and the State Teachers College under a unified University of Georgia with President Sanford as the head. This was the undoing of Soule, and the proud head of the Agriculture College resigned, ending twenty-six years of effective (but controversial) service to higher education and the state of Georgia.

Meanwhile, Richard B. Russell had become a United States Senator in 1932, and would represent the state and the country for thirty-eight years before his death in January 1971. During his long tenure he served as chairman of the powerful Armed Services Committee and president pro tempore of the Senate. All the while he was a strong supporter of the University. I had the pleasure of his company on several occasions as a young coach and was always impressed with his great enthusiasm for the University. He often referred to himself as the "proverbial sophomore." I was amazed at his detailed knowledge of the football team in those early years, wondering how he was able to keep up with the Bulldogs considering his many responsibilities in Washington.

I especially remember his giving me a personal tour of the Senate Chamber while he was president pro tempore. I was fascinated with the history and tradition of the Senate desks. To jog my memory as I wrote this book I spoke with Senator Johnny Isakson, who sent me an intriguing history of the Senate desk. Most all of the desks are small, some dating to the 1800s, and all are now numbered 1 through 100 representing the fifty states. I was surprised to learn that it is a tradition of the Senate for those in office to carve their names on their assigned desk, which could vary with each session based on longevity. For instance, during the course of his thirty-eight years in the senate, Russell occupied eight different desks, with his name carved on each one. At one time, Russell occupied desk 32, which has been occupied by Senators Herman E. Talmadge, Zell B. Miller, and current Senator Saxby Chambliss, all Georgia graduates. Of further interest is the fact that Russell later occupied desk 85, which was also occupied by current Senator Johnny Isakson, a Georgia graduate. The desk signing practice of these distinguished senators throughout history never ceases to amaze me.

Senator Russell returned to the University many times, and on one such occasion was honored by the Blue Key Honor Society, where I first met him. As the new, young football coach I was asked to say a few words at the first Blue Key Honors banquet in old Memorial Hall. I have a photograph inscribed by Senator Russell of him and me on that occasion. Also in the photograph are two of the founders of the Blue Key banquet, Buddy Darden, a University law student at the time and later United States representative from Marietta, and the late Tucker Dorsey, also a law school student who was killed in an auto accident shortly thereafter. Tucker was the son of Jasper Dorsey one of the University's greatest supporters. A memorial scholarship is given each year at the Blue Key banquet in Tucker Dorsey's name. The Blue Key Honors banquet is still in existence some fifty years later.

Senator Russell's papers are housed at the Richard B. Russell Memorial Library for Research and Studies located at the base of the main University library. They will be moved to the new Special Collections Library scheduled to open in 2012. The Russell Hall dormitory at the University is also named after the late Senator, as well as the Russell Senate Office building in Washington.

While Russell had been a supporter of Sanford, the new governor, Eugene Talmadge, elected in 1932, would

The Varsity restaurant opened on the corner across from the Arch in 1932.

prove to be a challenge not only to Sanford but to the entire system of public higher education in Georgia.

The Cocking Affair

When state law prevented Governor Talmadge from running for a third term in 1937 (terms then were two years), Eurith D. Rivers, a Roosevelt New Dealer, was elected. This was good news for the University. Federal funds had long been blocked by Talmadge, who was a bitter opponent of Roosevelt and the New Deal. With Talmadge gone a more liberal group of administrators

and teachers began to emerge in Georgia.

Foremost among those "forward thinkers" (or "radicals" to the followers of Talmadge) was Walter D. Cocking. He received his PhD from Columbia, and became Dean of Education at the University after Talmadge left office. Cocking received funding from the Julius Rosenwald Foundation of New York, whose mission was the promotion of social issues, especially the education of blacks. The Rosenwald fund was looked upon by conservative Talmadgites as "race mixing," "outside meddling," and "foreign ideas." Another beneficiary of the liberal foundation was Marvin S. Pittman; president of Georgia State Teachers College in Statesboro. Pittman had also received his PhD from Columbia and like Cocking was looked upon as a northern liberal.

When Talmadge and the conservatives returned to power in 1940 the clash of ideologies took center stage. Talmadge launched a head-on assault against the liberal element that had "infiltrated higher education in Georgia." The clash became known as "The Cocking Affair."

At the May 30, 1941, meeting of the Board of Regents in Athens, Georgia, Talmadge, as a voting member, announced that the Committee of Education and Finance had voted not to reelect Pittman as president. Talmadge then turned to Cocking and announced to the board he "would remove any person in the university system advocating communism or racial equality." Talmadge then moved that Dean Cocking not be reelected, and the board voted eight to four in favor of the governor's recommendation.

During a recess of the board, University President Harmon W. Caldwell was informed of the earlier events and immediately wrote a letter saying he would resign unless Cocking and Pittman were granted a hearing. When the board reassembled, chairman Sandy Beaver read President Caldwell's letter and suggested that Cocking and Pittman, in fairness, should be given a hearing prior to their removal. Most all the board approved despite Talmadge's vote against it. A board meeting was held the next month, and after testimony from both sides the board voted eight to seven to reappoint Cocking. A separate meeting was set for Pittman's case to be reviewed. Talmadge, who was "visibly upset" at the Cocking vote, went to work, and in a short period of time got three board members to resign and replaced them with people more favorable to his thinking. After a hearing with "trumped up charges" against Pittman and Cocking, the Talmadge-stacked board voted ten to five not to renew the two educators. The decision set off a huge backlash from the press and many Georgians.

The General Education Board immediately cut off aid to the University, and there were threats from accrediting agencies that schools of the university system would be "black-listed." Great discord erupted among the students of the system, and at the University a gathering of over one thousand hanged Talmadge in effigy. Such hangings were a popular student protest in those days.

Football coaches, I might add, were also the victims of outward student displeasures during my earlier career at Georgia. It was often said among those in our profession that you did not become a full-fledged coach unless you had been hung in effigy at least once. I qualified in 1967, my fourth year, after losing to Florida. But a forgiving student body was in high praise the next week after upsetting Auburn in Athens. Fortunately the hanging fad ended, but innovative students found other means of expressing displeasure. Meanwhile, the Talmadge crisis grew worse.

There were several other higher education personnel who fell victim to the "Talmadge Purge," including J. Curtis Dixon, vice chancellor of the system and leading critic of his boss, Chancellor Sanford. Curtis said Sanford was in a position to prevent the purges…but "chose a safe course rather than confront the governor." At that point Sanford thought it best to keep a low profile and not offend the governor.

General Sandy Beaver, Board of Regents chair and head of the Riverside Military Academy, tried to resolve the crisis with a proposed compromise between Talmadge and the accrediting agencies. Beaver, a University graduate and football letterman in 1901-1902, was a boyhood friend of Governor Talmadge and a staunch supporter. Beaver served as Talmadge's chief of staff, and the governor gave Beaver the title of "general." Beaver said, "I would crawl on my belly to restore recognition of schools." Talmadge was in no mood to compromise. In fact, he was furious and "went into a tantrum" when he read Beaver's statement in the paper. He called for Beaver's resignation, declaring "Georgia don't want any chairman of the Board of Regents crawling on his belly!"

Despite that tirade, Beaver must have convinced Talmadge it was wise politically to back off for the good of education in the state and to admit he "had inadvertently run afoul of the higher education system." The accrediting committee investigating the entire debacle was not impressed with Talmadge's remorsefulness, and upon the committee's recommendation, 400 of the Southern Association members at its meeting in Louisville in December, 1941, voted unanimously to remove the University of Georgia from the list of accredited members.

The accrediting association further announced that

Governor Eugene Talmadge (second from left) and President Steadman V. Sanford (second from right)

the Georgia constitution should be rewritten to "place the university system beyond control of any governor… and that every school in the university system (except Negro schools) would be stripped of accredited status." The action by the Southern Association would be effective in the fall of 1942, thus throwing the issue into the gubernatorial election that November. Talmadge's opponent, Ellis G. Arnall, a graduate of the UGA law school, based his campaign on education and pledged to accede to every demand made by the accrediting agency.

Immediately thereafter Beaver resigned as chief of Governor Talmadge's staff and as a regent came out in support of Arnall. Shortly thereafter Chancellor Sanford, who had kept a diplomatic low profile during the earlier storm, came out in support of Arnall.

Arnall won handily, and after taking office, the General Assembly passed a constitutional amendment, ratified by vote of the people, removing the governor from the Board of Regents of the university system and from the State Board of Education. The new Board of Regents invited Marvin Pittman to once again become president of Georgia Teachers College. Cocking was also invited to return as education dean at Georgia, but he declined. In the spring of 1943, the Southern Association of College and Schools restored accreditation to the University and to the system.

While the University System of Georgia and its flagship institution survived its most serious crisis, the resolution came with a high price. The reputations of the system and the University were badly damaged. The press had a field day ridiculing the state and higher education as "backwards and racist." Enrollment in 1942 also suffered "plummeting to 37 percent below the 1940 level." However, the enormous drop in enrollment cannot be attributed solely to the Talmadge debacle. World War II took its toll on college enrollment at the University and colleges throughout the country. Once again the University and many of its students went to war, this time across the two great waters, the Atlantic and Pacific.

Terrell Hall

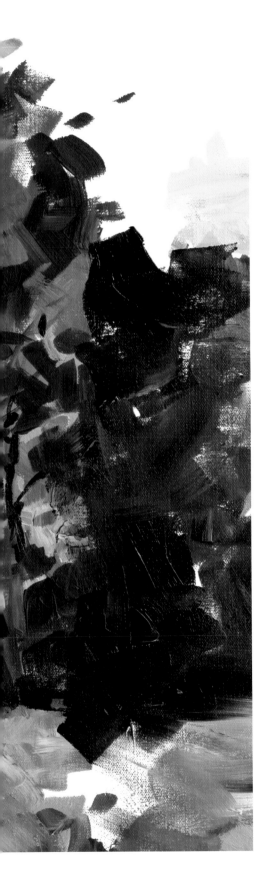

WAR YEARS AND BEYOND

Most every person living and old enough to remember knows where they were on Sunday December 7, 1941, the "day that will live in infamy." I was nine years old sitting in a drugstore on Dauphine Street in Mobile, Alabama, at 1 PM drinking a Coca-Cola with a group of elderly men. They gathered around the radio stunned while listening to news of the Japanese bombing of Pearl Harbor. I was there waiting and listening until it was time to walk across the street to the Cathedral of Immaculate Conception, where I would serve as an altar boy at the exposition of the Blessed Sacrament on that day of adoration.

While I was not aware of what was happening at the University of Georgia, I was very much aware of the school through its All-American football players, Frank Sinkwich, Charley Trippi, and Herb St. John. I had cut their pictures out of the newspaper and put them in my scrapbook. Later I learned how the University was affected by World War II.

Almost immediately after Pearl Harbor, there began a steady decrease in the University's enrollment as many young men enlisted in or were drafted into the armed forces. During the war years, enrollment steadily dropped from a high of 3,600-plus hundred to about 2,000, eventually leaving only

Frank Sinkwich

about 1,500-plus students on campus. Of that number, the majority were women, which marked the first time in the school's history that happened, but it would not be the last.

The small enrollment however was supplemented by an influx of some 6,000 military trainees a year from around the country. Thanks to the influence of University alumni, Senator Richard B. Russell and Congressman Carl Vinson, Georgia was selected as one of the

five schools in the nation for naval preflight training. From 1942 to 1945, approximately 20,000 navy cadets trained at the University in basic military procedures. Interestingly, among the trainees was the soon-to-be famous college football coach Paul W. "Bear" Bryant. Bear's stay on the Georgia campus was short, however. Madison A. "Matty" Bell, Hall of Fame football coach and later athletic director at SMU, who was an officer in the preflight school at the time, told me he had to ship

Bryant out after a perceived personal indiscretion that caused a serious confrontation with a fellow trainee. Bell said, "I shipped the Bear one way and the other trainee the other way." Any details of the experiences of the "Bear" in Bulldog country were buried in the navy files. Bear Bryant did return to the University on several occasions in the 1960s and 1970s with his powerful Alabama football teams.

To accommodate the large influx of trainees, the navy took over many campus buildings such as Baldwin, Memorial, Woodruff, and Snelling Halls. In addition, the navy built several new buildings and athletic facilities that they left after the war. The facilities became part of the campus landscape for many years. The old Stegeman Hall gym/swimming pool served two generations of male students. The field house and the four practice fields nearby were also left and served Georgia athletics for many years. The field house was a dressing facility for the Georgia football team until I arrived, when it was replaced by the Georgia (Stegeman) Coliseum. The old field house later became the alumni house that was eventually torn down and replaced by the current Rankin Smith Sr. Student-Athlete Achievement Center. The athletic facilities left by the navy were a boost to the football team, which became a powerhouse during the decade of the 1940s, under Wallace A. "Wally" Butts, who coached the Bulldogs for twenty-two years.

Ole Miss had earlier persuaded Harry Mehre, the successful Georgia coach of the 1930s, to come to Oxford as head coach. Mehre later became a popular sportswriting analyst for *The Atlanta Journal* after he was fired by Ole Miss. Mehre had a great sense of humor and often told the story that Ole Miss gave him "a lifetime contract" that persuaded him to leave Georgia. After several struggling years at Ole Miss they "declared me legally dead and fired me!"

Wally Butts Jr., a Mercer graduate and Milledgeville native, led the Bulldogs to four Southeastern Conference championships and a national championship during his twenty-two years as coach. Three of those championships were in the 1940s (1942, '46, '48) with the 1942 team being declared national champions by several polls. The undefeated 1946 team was also selected as a national champion by the Williamson Poll.

Butts coached two of the greatest college football players in the history of the game: Frank Sinkwich and Charley Trippi. Sinkwich won the Heisman Trophy in 1942, and Trippi the Maxwell Trophy in 1946. Trippi, I believe, is the best all-around back in college football history. That opinion was shared by the late Bobby Dodd of Georgia Tech and Harry Gilmer of Alabama fame. Both Sinkwich and Trippi were heroes of mine growing up, and I was in awe when I first met them upon my arrival at the University in 1963 as the head coach at the tender age of thirty-one.

Coach Butts also served as athletic director, and while he was a great football coach, he was not as proficient as an administrator. Despite the success of the football team, the Athletic Association was constantly in financial difficulty. It became even more of a problem in the 1950s, as his teams suffered through five losing seasons during the decade. The one bright spot was the 1959 championship team, led by Fran Tarkenton. That success was followed by a 6-4 record in 1960, however, and Coach Butts resigned as head coach, and remained as athletic director until 1962. He had the good fortune to finish with a four-year win streak over the "ancient enemy," Georgia Tech.

When I arrived in Athens in December 1963, Coach Butts was involved in a scandal that rocked the University and college football. Bear Bryant, head coach at the University of Alabama, and Butts still athletic director, were accused in an article published by the *Saturday Evening Post* in March 1963 of fixing the football game between Georgia and Alabama on September 22, 1962, which Alabama won 35-0. The Post reported that George Burnett, an insurance agent from Atlanta "overheard a critical long-distance call" between Butts and Bryant on September 14, just eight days before the game. The Post, with Burnett as the source, stated that Butts "outlined Georgia's offensive plays to Bryant and told him how Georgia plans to defend Alabama's attack." The story coincided with the controversial departure of Butts as athletic director from Georgia. I was advised when I came not to associate with Coach Butts, but I thought otherwise. I knew nothing about the scandal, but I did know Coach Butts from afar as a great football coach. So I went to see him shortly after I arrived to pay my respects. Coach Butts never forgot the gesture during those difficult times and was a strong supporter of mine the rest of his life.

He and Coach Bryant sued the *Post* and won set-

Coach Wally Butts

tlements against the magazine. A jury awarded Coach Butts a $3.06 million judgment, which the judge reduced to $460,000, and Bryant settled with the magazine for a $300,000 tax-free arrangement. The financial situation of the Athletic Association, meanwhile, remained a constant problem until the arrival of Joel Eaves, the former Auburn basketball coach, who became athletic director and started the process of developing a fiscally sound operation.

Much of Coach Butts' success in the '40s was with football players recruited from the North. Coach Butts was a demanding taskmaster, and his rough discipline tactics were ideally suited for the many hardcore war veterans who played on the team. While many football players and students returned after the war, many others never returned. It is estimated that about 200 Georgia students paid the ultimate sacrifice for victory in World War II. That number included some fifteen student-athletes, Henry T. Elrod of Rebecca, Georgia, among them, who won the Medal of Honor early in the war in defense of Wake Island, the first marine pilot to be so honored.

Fran Tarkenton

Butts-Mehre Heritage Hall

Memorable tributes on campus honor the University students who died in all the wars fought by the United States. The memorial to all the Georgia students is located by the Student Learning Center on North Campus. There is also a memorial to the student-athletes across from the Smith Academic Center adjacent to the football practice fields.

When the war was over, the University, like institutions throughout the country, was flooded with veterans, most taking advantage of the G.I. Education Bill. In the academic year 1945-46, enrollment increased almost 97 percent at Georgia, and by 1948 nearly 8,000 were enrolled in the University. That number stabilized and then dropped by the end of the decade.

President Harmon W. Caldwell, who served the University for thirteen years before becoming chancellor in 1948, is given high marks in leading the University during the difficult times of the Cocking Affair, and the war and post-war challenges. Historian Thomas G. Dyer credited Caldwell with starting the institution toward a "slow modernization of the University's missions of teaching, research, and public service." Dyer also pointed out that the University "had begun to win some recognition as a result of talented faculty members who had strong national reputations," such as artist Lamar Dodd and historian E. Merton Coulter. I will always remember retired Professor Coulter making the inspiring statement in his latter years that he would

Lamar Dodd

rather "wear out than rust out." He was very active and productive until his death in 1981. Dodd, meanwhile, inspired all who knew him at the University, and his many contributions led to the naming of the art school in his honor in 1996. He headed the art department for forty years and gained a national reputation as an administrator and distinguished artist. And like Coulter, he was active and productive all of his life. Barbara and I are proud to have several Dodd originals, especially one called "The Happening," a painting of the celebration on the field at the Sugar Bowl after beating Notre Dame in 1980 to win the national championship. Stalwarts such as Coulter, Dodd, and others provided a strong faculty base for Omer Clyde (O.C.) Aderhold,

who became president in 1950 and guided the University through tremendous growth and dramatic changes in the years ahead.

Omer Clyde "O.C." Aderhold

On December 4, 1963, University President Omer Clyde "O.C." Aderhold announced, to the shock of the Bulldog Nation, that I would become the head football coach at the University of Georgia. President Aderhold had put his faith in the new athletic director, Joel Eaves, a former Auburn basketball coach who had been given the charge of unilaterally running the chaotic athletic program. Eaves was given sole power to search for and hire the head football coach to replace Johnny Griffith, who resigned in 1963. Eaves, in a shocking decision, hired me, a thirty-one year old unknown freshmen football coach from the rival school of Auburn. As an administrator, which I was later in my career for twenty-five years, there is no way I would have hired myself with those qualifications. Only the most loyal of Georgia supporters were excited about the hire. I have often said that looking back on it now, only Eaves, my wife, Barbara, and I thought it was a good decision.

At the time, I knew very little about Georgia and nothing about President Aderhold. As a matter of fact, when Barbara and I were going through a receiving line at an introductory party held for us, Dr. Aderhold introduced himself to Barbara as "O.C. Aderhold." Barbara, who was a twenty-four year old coach's wife, responded in her naïve effervescent way, "Great to meet you O.C. What do you do?" I choked awkwardly doing my best to rectify the situation! Aderhold was gracious and got a kick out of the comment.

I did come to know President O.C. Aderhold as a gentleman of the highest order who would lead the University for seventeen years. He accomplished much for the University, but toward the latter part of his reign he experienced some of the most tumultuous years in the University's history.

Aderhold, a Georgia alumnus from Lavonia, had received his PhD from Ohio State and eventually became dean of the University of Georgia College of Education. He was named president of the University in 1950, following the short reign of Jonathan C. Rogers, who served less than two years. Rogers' short term as president was mainly focused on a power struggle with agriculture Dean Harry Brown who wanted the college separated from the University. Rogers was able to work with the Board of Regents persuading them to centralize control at the University. The new arrangement required the agriculture dean to coordinate the extension service and the experiment stations reporting ultimately to the University president. Rogers' victory was costly, however, as both he and Brown resigned under pressure, which opened the way for Aderhold to become president and C.C. Murray became the agriculture dean. Aderhold and Murray worked well together for many years.

UGA Agriculture: "The State Is Our Campus"

When I arrived at the University in 1964, I immediately searched for ways to utilize the University's state outreach programs to help realize my goal of dominating the state in recruiting student-athletes. I found that resource in the cooperative extension service, which had county agents in all of Georgia's 159 counties.

I arranged a visit with L.W. "Hoop" Eberhardt Jr., director of the UGA extension service. His office was in the Hoke Smith Building, near the football practice fields and the Stegeman Coliseum. The Smith Building is appropriately named after two-time Georgia governor (1907-09, 1911) and United States Senator (1911-20) Michael Hoke Smith, who cosponsored the Smith-Lever Act of 1914 (Asbury F. Lever, U.S. Representative from South Carolina) establishing the cooperative extension service nationwide. The act provided federal money with matching state and county funding to bring education to rural communities through demonstrations and practical application.

I met with Eberhardt and asked for his help in establishing a recruiting network with the county agents throughout the state. Eberhardt, a 1936 UGA forestry graduate and staunch Bulldog, was sold on the idea and arranged for me to meet with all the county agents at their annual meeting at the 4-H camp at Rock Eagle, just outside Eatonton, Georgia.

Eberhardt, who apparently ran the organization with an iron fist, introduced me, reminding the agents that they were employees of the University of Georgia and were expected to help me in my recruiting goals. While most of the agents were

Chapel

Bulldog fans, I often wondered how those few agents whose alma maters were Clemson or Auburn felt about the Eberhardt dictate. Needless to say, I avoided calling on them directly for help.

I am indebted to the county agents who helped this neophyte coach get off to a much-needed good start. I also remain indebted to Hoop Eberhardt, who became a longtime friend and supporter and led an inspiring life, devoted to his alma mater while living in Athens until his death in 2004 at ninety-one.

I also had the privilege to visit the University's two main experimental stations in Griffin and Tifton. The Griffin campus was established in 1888 by the Hatch Act, which gave federal land grants to states for agricultural experiment stations. The campus has long provided research, extension and teaching to the Piedmont and North Georgia sections of the state. The many services provided by the station through the years have had a significant impact on a variety of agribusiness operations.

I visited the Griffin campus (123 acres) with horticulture guru Dr. Michael Dirr, who was evaluating the station's collection of shrubs and trees. The campus, which totals almost 500 acres, now offers classes for undergraduate students, and as of 2010, has an enrollment of eighteen students. In 2005, Spalding County residents passed a S.P.L.O.S.T initiative that included funds for a $10 million student learning center for the UGA Griffin campus.

Meanwhile the Tifton campus, farther south, opened its doors in 1919 and is proud to make the claim of being the first coastal plains experiment station in the nation. UGA researchers have formed an ongoing partnership with the U.S. Department of Agriculture research service that dates from 1924. The Tifton campus has 350 UGA employees, plus 95 USDA employees.

The campus is also home to 100 graduate and undergraduate students. The Tifton website proudly claims that "students attending classes on the UGA campus can earn a UGA bachelor of science in agriculture without stepping a foot in Athens."

I visited the arboretum at the Tifton campus and watched with special interest Dr. John M. Ruter's good horticultural works with conifers and new ornamentals. Ruter, who has introduced and patented several plants, will leave the Tifton campus in the fall of 2012 to accept the Allan Armitage Endowed Professorship at the UGA Athens campus.

My last visit to the Tifton campus was in the spring of 2011, when I spoke at the request of Angie Hunt, a former UGA student, to a Tifton library foundation fund raiser. The event was held at the impressive John Hunt Conference Center named in memory of Angie's late father-in-law. Hunt was a highly respected Tifton businessman and philanthropist and member of the university system's Board of Regents and was the one most responsible for securing the conference center on the Tifton campus. Hunt's charming wife, Julie, served on the Board of Regents after her husband's passing and currently is serving on the UGA Foundation, while her son Dallas runs the family business.

While visiting the campus I was impressed with the dual pride of the citizens in the "Tifton UGA campus." I later found out they have their own unique Bulldog mascot named "TUGA," whose caricature is depicted wearing a red Tifton campus hat with the UGA arch emblem, sporting sunglasses and a protruding single fang and smirky smile. My immediate thought was, "Go TUGA Dawg!"

Having the College of Agriculture and Environmental Science and the extension service and the two main experiment stations and numerous substations all under one umbrella ultimately reporting to the University president was a good way for Dr. O.C. Aderhold to begin his term in office.

Aderhold: Moving Toward a Modern University

Aderhold kicked off his presidency in 1950 by proudly watching the College of Veterinary Medicine (restarted in 1946) graduate its first class the same year it was accredited. The following year the vet school's first permanent building was opened, and the school grew rapidly into a first-class program especially with the support of Fred Davison, a doctor of veterinary medicine, dean of the Vet School, and later University president beginning in 1966. The Georgia veterinarians soon balanced the many south Georgia vet doctors who attended the Auburn veterinary school at the "loveliest village," since that had been their close-by option at the time. The

Ilah Dunlap Little Memorial Library

many Auburn vet doctors had been great football recruiters in South Georgia for their school, so I was glad to see the emergence of veterinarians from Georgia.

President Aderhold was most proud of his accomplishments of bringing to the University an elaborate science center on Ag Hill. In the complex there were buildings for chemistry, physics, geology, the biological sciences, food science and animal science. In my early years at Georgia, President Aderhold often bragged about the science center that was finished in 1960. He proudly drove me by the facilities one day pointing out each building and the discipline it represented. He was also proud that in 1955 the Kellogg Foundation made a $2.5 million grant to build the Georgia Center for Continuing Education. The Center was an enormous boost, bringing a multitude of conferences to the University from all over the Southeast. We used the facility in the early years as an impressive recruiting headquarters on game day.

Aderhold also saw during his early tenure in 1953 the completion of the Ilah Dunlap Little Memorial Library. The new facility provided much-needed space at the time, to meet the ever-expanding volumes housed in the old library that was built in 1905. In time the new library outgrew itself, so an annex was completed in 1974. Today a magnificent $42 million special collections library has been constructed. Included in the new facility are the Hargrett Rare Book and Manuscript Library, the Richard B. Russell Library, and the Walter J. Brown Archives and The Peabody Awards Collection.

The library has a special place in my heart at the University. Barbara and I made a substantial gift to the library that was used as seed money to start a $1 million endowment fundraiser that I was proud to chair. We actually doubled the goal, and today the $2.5 million endowment annually provides funds that are used by the library for acquiring special materials. An example is the acquisition of papers from notables such as former Georgia Governor Sonny Perdue, who played on the Georgia freshman football team in 1965.

After the library holdings were moved (1953) to the new Dunlap Little facility, the old library building was renovated and became the Georgia Museum of Art. The building served the art museum from 1958 until it moved to its new East Campus facility in 1996. When the museum left, the building was renovated once again and today serves as the central office for the administrative staff of the University.

In 1954 Aderhold worked with two distinguished University alumni, powerful Congressman Carl Vinson and Senator Richard Russell, to persuade the United States Navy to buy the old State Normal School campus and to locate its supply corps school on the site. It was

The Iron Horse

a tremendous deal for the University and a bonanza for the Athens community. More than 400 young officers graduated from the basic six-month course each year. Some socialized with University coeds and ended up marrying them, establishing a permanent connection to Athens and the University. Among the most noted of the Supply Corps graduates was Roger Staubach, Naval Academy Heisman Trophy winner, Dallas Cowboy superstar, and college and pro football Hall of Famer. Staubach often came to the practice fields after classes to work out. As an ultrasuccessful Dallas businessman, he still recalls fondly his time spent in Athens and at the University. He proudly proclaims that his first child was born in the Classic City.

Ironically, fifty-five years later the navy closed the Supply Corps School and transferred the property back to the University for the establishment of a health sciences campus. The first class of forty medical students was enrolled in August 2010 in the interim medical partnership building on campus while the old navy campus was being transformed. The partnership between the Medical College of Georgia and the University was created to educate more physicians for the state.

In his early years as president, Aderhold had his campus challenges, highlighted by a rather bizarre incident. On May 24, 1954, a giant metal abstract sculpture of a horse appeared on the lawn of one of the student housing areas called Reed Quadrangle. The strange looking monstrosity, which came to be known as the "Iron Horse," was created by Abott Pattison, a visiting artist from Chicago, and immediately became the target of a storm of protest by the students. By that evening some 500 rowdy students gathered and proceeded to deface the sculpture in various ways, and then they attempted to set it on fire and marched around it with torches chanting "burn the horse." The next day the art faculty met and voiced support for the artist, but Aderhold, moved by rumors it might be dynamited, ordered the sculpture removed from the campus.

After a circuitous journey the Iron Horse ended up on top of a hill on a cornfield farm of retired University Professor Lawrence C. Curtis, where it still remains. It can be seen today on Highway 15 just north of the bridge over the Oconee River near Greensboro. Through the years it has become the subject of many articles,

films, and fables. I, like so many others who have traveled the highway, always look for the Iron Horse, relating some fictitious story of its history, as I have done so often with my children and grandchildren.

Despite such frivolous interruptions, the University under President Aderhold made tremendous strides toward becoming a modern university. However, there were dark clouds hovering over the school with the football program, and even darker clouds during the early days of integration in 1961.

Integration

In September 1950 Horace Ward from Atlanta applied for admission to the University of Georgia School of Law, becoming the first African American to attempt to break the segregation policy of the University. Ward, with the assistance and guidance of the NAACP, tried for six years to break the racial barrier at the University. After many delays and strategic maneuvering, the University officially denied Ward's application. The decision was upheld in federal courts. Ward eventually enrolled at Northwestern University and later became the first African American to serve on the federal bench in Georgia. Ironically, Ward presided over several cases involving the University, including the highly publicized Jan Kemp lawsuit. The earlier efforts by Ward and others to break the racial barrier at the University in the 1950s paved the way for the eventual integration of the school. It would not come easy, however.

Like other schools in the South, Georgia was determined to resist the United States Supreme Court ruling of 1954 in the *Brown v. Board of Education* case, which declared segregation unconstitutional in public education. Nevertheless, in 1961 the University, under court order, admitted the first black students in its history, Charlayne Hunter and Hamilton Holmes. They transferred in as juniors. Briefly, the now-integrated University was peaceful, but deep-seated prejudices quietly smoldered among many of the students. Passion erupted on the night of the second day of classes. After an emotional basketball loss to arch rival Georgia Tech, at old Woodruff Hall a group of students left the arena and headed for Myers Hall, where Charlayne

Hunter was living. By the time the crowd arrived at the dorm, it had grown to several hundred and turned into a riotous mob. Obscenities were shouted, bricks, rocks, and bottles were thrown, windows were broken, and a banner was waved reading "Nigger Go Home." Athens police and old reliable Dean of Men William Tate kept the mob at bay for a while, but stronger measures had to be used. Finally tear gas and water hoses quelled the mob. Shortly after the crowd had dispersed, Dean of Students Joseph A. Williams decided, for safety precautions, to remove the black students. Holmes and Hunter were taken back to Atlanta by the state patrol that night. After much discussion among state and University officials, reason prevailed, and Holmes and Hunter returned to class five days later to a much calmer University.

Two years later both Holmes and Hunter graduated, and each had successful careers. Holmes became a respected orthopedic surgeon, and Hunter a renowned journalist. In pursuit of his medical degree, Holmes became the first African American student to attend and receive his MD from the Emory University School of Medicine.

Dr. Holmes, a delightful gentleman, became a big supporter of our athletic program, often helping with recruiting, especially black student-athletes. Holmes had played football in high school, and his son, Hamilton E. Holmes Jr., was a walk-on for our freshman team in 1986. The younger Holmes graduated from the University in 1990.

It was through communicating with Charlayne Hunter-Gault in South Africa that I first became aware of how fast technology has shrunk the modern world. As one who has moved very slowly into this new world of technology, I emailed her in South Africa congratulating her when the academic building was named in her and Dr. Holmes' honor. Expecting to hear from her in a couple of weeks (if at all), I received a return email in ten minutes! I was amazed! I couldn't believe that technology had made our world so small.

Dr. Holmes died of heart failure in 1995, but Char-layne Hunter-Gault has returned often from South Africa to the campus for special events. She was the commencement speaker in 1988 on the twenty-fifth anniversary of her graduation. She also returned January 9, 2001, for the forty-year celebration of the integration of the University and the naming of the Hunter-Holmes Academic Building. It was in the academic building, near "the Arch," that Holmes and Hunter on January 9, 1961, had registered for classes at the University. Hunter-Gault returned again in January 2011, for the fifty-year celebration of the integration of the University. As part of the half-century celebration, a re-enactment of the legal trial that desegregated the University was held. Also as part of the celebration Mary Frances Early, the University's first African American graduate earning a master's of music education degree in 1962, spoke at the annual Freedom Breakfast held at the University. I visited with her shortly thereafter at the Southeast Flower Show. She was very proud of her association with the University and her role as the first African American to graduate from the college.

I also had the privilege of communicating with another African American pioneer in the integration of the University. Dr. Harold Black, who in 1962 became the first African American to enroll in the Terry College of Business and the first black male to live in a UGA residence hall, wrote to me in 2010 from the University of Tennessee expressing his pleasure with my son Derek's becoming the head football coach at that institution. At the time I knew little of Dr. Black's significant role in the integration of UGA and his achievement as a Distinguished Professor at the University of Tennessee. For twenty-four years Dr. Black held the James H. Smith Jr. Professor of Financial Studies. He retired in 2011 but has returned often to the University of Georgia speaking about his part in the integration of the institution and how it impacted his career.

As part of the extended recognition of the fiftieth anniversary of the desegregation of the University, Hunter-Gault returned again to the campus in March 2011, this time to discuss her autobiography, *In My Place*,

Opposite page: Academic Building near the Arch

with students and faculty. She made a profound statement regarding the journalism school and her role as a journalist that is worth repeating: "In our journalism schools, we teach the term objectivity, which I am going to go on a crusade against. Your computer can be objective, because it doesn't have a heart. It doesn't have personal history. But all of us have hearts and personal histories, so we can't be objective. I prefer to say that we have to be journalists who are fair and balanced." This is the most profound observation I have heard of the role of journalists.

The Integration of Intercollegiate Athletics

With the integration of universities throughout the South taking place, it was only a matter of time before it happened in intercollegiate athletics. Kentucky, a border state during the Civil War, was the first school in the Southeast to sign an African American football player to a scholarship.

Harry Sims, from Athens, walked on for the track team in the 1968-69 season, marking the first black student athlete to compete at the University. Sims was later a teacher for many years in the Classic City and has for some twenty years served as a commissioner of Clarke County. Legendary head track coach Forrest "Spec" Towns had concerns about assigning roommates on road trips that season. However, assistant coach and former track star Lewis Gainey volunteered to room with Sims. Gainey, a loyal and dedicated employee, later became Georgia's head track coach and assistant athletic director for event management. Gainey said he didn't mind, and jokingly said, "Besides, it was a good excuse not to room with the chain-smoking Coach Towns," a habit fashionable at the time.

Maxie Foster, a 400-meter track competitor from Cedar Shoals High School in Athens, became the first black student-athlete to sign a scholarship grant-in-aid. Foster first competed in the 1969-70 school year and eventually earned his six-year degree in education. He taught for many years in the University of Louisiana Shreveport, and returned often to his hometown and visited the athletic department.

Credit goes to Towns and Gainey for taking the initiative in recruiting the first black student-athlete. The track and stadium are named in honor and memory of Spec Towns, the Georgia track star who achieved world fame in the sport. In 1937 at the Berlin Olympics, Towns won the gold medal in the 110-meter high hurdles. On the same trip a month later, Towns set the world record in Oslo, Norway, with the time of 13.7 seconds, a record that stood for fourteen years. My long-time overseas travelling companion and Athletic Association fund-raiser, historian, promoter, and football sideline reporter Loran Smith and I visited the track in Oslo where Towns broke the record. We wanted to see firsthand the site of the historic event and study the design of the stadium press box that we used as a model for building the Georgia track stadium named for Towns. Smith, a former Georgia track captain (1960), and I had fun acting like little kids jumping over a couple of hurdles re-enacting Spec setting the world record.

In 1968 James Hurley became the first African American to walk-on for football at the University. The players paid their respects to Hurley in the rugged "circle butt drill," but Hurley gained their respect by quietly but competitively responding to the challenge. Hurley left the University after spring practice to enroll at Vanderbilt on a football scholarship.

In 1971 we signed and enrolled the first five black football players at the University. There were three local players: Horace King, Clarence Pope, and Richard Appleby. King earned his degree and played nine years of professional football with the Detroit Lions and stayed in that city as an executive with General Motors, often returning to his hometown and alma mater. Pope stayed in Athens and became a minister and Athens firefighter, while Appleby (whose memorable touchdown pass to Gene Washington allowed the Bulldogs to upset Florida 10-7 in 1975) went to Hawaii to work with the state's

Opposite page: Hunter-Holmes Academic Building and iron fence erected around 1859

Richard Appleby passing to Gene Washington against Florida in 1975

airline. Larry West from Albany and Chuck Kinnebrew from Rome were also among the initial five black signees. Both graduated, and Kinnebrew became an executive with Westinghouse. West became a pastor of one of the largest Baptist churches in Washington, D.C. Four of the five were able to return to Athens to be recognized at a football game in 2001 on the thirtieth anniversary of their coming to Georgia to play football and pursue their education.

In the early 1960s, when President Aderhold was guiding the University through integration, he also found himself saddled with the Wally Butts controversy. Not long after we came to the University, Coach Butts, a gentle and kind-hearted man, came to our home while I was working and brought a dozen red roses to Barbara to welcome her to Georgia. Barbara told me, "Coach Butts is the sweetest man I've ever met." I smiled knowing that he was better known as a stern disciplinarian who had to train a rugged group of veterans returning from World War II. Some of those players would never have considered him a "sweet man."

Nevertheless, because of alleged indiscretions in his social life and poor financial judgment in his professional life, Butts was forced to step aside as head football coach and was replaced by the Georgia freshman coach, Johnny Griffith. Butts stayed on as athletic director but was forced to resign three years later when *The Saturday Evening Post* story accusations were published. Because of Butts' popularity with those loyal to "the coach" the issue set off a divisive controversy through-out the state. Aderhold, a gentle man with a wonderful wife, had known Butts for many years and was pained by the controversy. Caught between the pressure of integration and the indiscretions of the coach, Aderhold once told Dr. Fred Davison in a weak moment (pointing to his neck), he was "up to here with football coaches and integration radicals."

It was understandable why he seemed to be such a happy and relieved man in our early years at Georgia. The stress he had endured was eased considerably with the new administration of athletics. The Athletic Association became fiscally responsible under the management and leadership of the newly hired athletic director Joel Eaves, a respected man of integrity. At the same time, our scrappy football team had some big wins, beating Florida and Georgia Tech and going to the Sun Bowl, thereby rallying the support of the student body and once skeptical alumni and supporters. I remember sitting by a swimming pool with a happy and relieved President Aderhold in El Paso, Texas, at the Sun Bowl. He thanked and congratulated me for the success of the 1964 team. He was even happier when we beat Texas Tech in the bowl. By the third year in 1966, we won the Southeastern Conference Championship. Perhaps that success may have contributed to a very tired Dr. Aderhold announcing his decision to retire the following year. I had the privilege of serving the University for forty years. Of those many years, none were more enjoyable than those early years at Georgia under President Aderhold.

The Georgia Redcoat Marching Band

THE BEST AND WORST OF TIMES

The University was fortunate to have back-to-back long-tenured presidents who were loyal alumni with deep affection for their alma mater. Both were members of the Rotary Club of Athens, and they both espoused the Rotary motto of "Service Above Self" concerning their University.

Both Davison and his future wife, Dianne, finished the vet school at the University in 1952. Davison practiced vet medicine in Marietta for several years before pursuing further studies. He received his PhD from Iowa State in 1963, and was appointed dean of the vet school at Georgia shortly thereafter. It was during the time Davison was dean that I first met him at a University function. I found him to be pleasant, outgoing, with real interest in the football program at Georgia.

In 1966 Davison moved to Atlanta as vice chancellor of the system and returned to Athens the following year as president of the University. His long tenure at Georgia (nineteen years) was in many ways, as Charles Dickens wrote in *A Tale of Two Cities,* "the best of times" and sadly, in the last years, "the worst of times."

Best of Times

Davison arrived at the University in 1967, when state support for higher education was at an all-time high. Much of the credit should go to the leadership of Governor Carl Sanders, a Georgia alumnus from Augusta who attended Georgia on a football scholarship in 1942. Sanders was a bomber pilot in World War II before returning to the University to earn his undergraduate degree and then his law degree (L.L.B 1948). This earned him the distinction of "Double Dawg" status. He was responsible for the construction of an addition to the law school (authorized in 1963 and completed in 1967), composed primarily of an elaborate law library.

At the dedication Governor Sanders had the following to say about this proud moment for the state of Georgia and its citizens: "The people of Georgia want and deserve nothing short of the best. The University of Georgia School of Law is, therefore, to be one of such excellence that no citizen of Georgia need ever leave his state because a superior legal education is available elsewhere." The quote is inscribed on the wall of the library addition.

Governor Sanders was very interested as well in the football program. After the war he lettered in 1945 and played in the 1946 Oil Bowl in Houston, Texas. He wanted Georgia to maintain a quality program. He was very helpful to me when I first arrived. In order to compete in the rugged Southeastern Conference in those days an athletic dorm was high priority. Because of bad experiences with an athletic dorm, the administration had done away with the one at the University after Butts resigned. Thanks to Governor Sanders' support, a new athletic dorm was built which provided us with an important recruiting tool. Speaking of recruiting, Governor Sanders helped us recruit key athletes, advising Georgia prospects to "stay in the state."

Davison benefited from Sanders' support of higher education, and during his first year as president the University received from the state $34 million, a remarkable 70 percent increase from the previous year. Enrollment also soared to over 23,000. To meet the need of the expanding student body, an additional 450 faculty members were hired, bringing the total to some 2,000.

Governor Carl Sanders

By the mid-1980s the University had a budget of $225 million of which $119 million came from state appropriations. Of special note is the tremendous growth in expenditure on research programs. After the war only $168,000 was expended in support of research programs, and by the mid-1980s nearly $75 million was spent in support of a multitude of programs benefiting the state and nation. At the forefront of this incredible emphasis on research were some of the "world's most prominent geneticists, biologists and chemists on its faculty" as well as world-renowned professors in a multitude of disciplines.

Distinguished Professors

In July 1984, the University, under Davison, started the yearlong celebration of its two hundredth birthday with a series of special events highlighted by Vice President George H. W. Bush's delivering one of the bicentennial addresses. Honored at the occasions were five of the University's most distinguished faculty members. Each received a special sterling silver bicentennial medallion. All five had achieved national and international acclaim, bringing prestige to the University. Certainly this is an outstanding starting lineup: Glenn W. Burton (agronomy), Lamar Dodd (art), Norman H. Giles (genetics), Eugene P. Odum (ecology), and Dean Rusk (law).

Burton, who worked at the University's campus in Tifton after receiving his PhD at Rutgers (1938), became one of the world's foremost agricultural scientists. He developed hybrid grasses used in countries around the world and on most athletic fields, including Sanford Stadium.

Giles, from Atlanta, received his PhD in biology from Harvard and later taught at Yale. While at Yale, he gained an international reputation as an authority in genetics. He returned to his home state in 1972 with his Yale research team to direct the Department of Molecular and Population Genetics at the University. He was later inducted in the National Academy of Science.

Dodd, from LaGrange, emerged as a nationally known artist and became a highly respected administrator while directing the Art School at the University for forty years. In 1995 the Art School was appropriately named in his honor.

Thanks to the pioneering work of Odum, the Institute of Ecology was established at the University in 1966. Odum devoted his life to this "new discipline," which earned him the title "father of ecology."

In 1970, President Davison recruited Dean Rusk to join the faculty as the Samuel Sibley Professor of International and Comparative Law. Rusk grew up in Cherokee County and attended Boys' High School in Atlanta, Davidson College, and later St. John's College in Oxford as a Rhodes Scholar. He earned his law degree from the University of California at Berkeley and served as Secretary of State under John F. Kennedy and Lyndon B. Johnson. The hiring of Rusk at the University

Dean Rusk

was controversial at the time. A still very conservative Georgia frowned on the fact that Rusk's daughter had married a black classmate at Stanford University, and some liberals denounced his Vietnam policy. Roy Harris, a strong segregationist and a member of the Board of Regents, denounced the appointment because of the "mixed marriage." Nevertheless, the hiring of Rusk turned out to be one of Davison's greatest decisions. The former secretary of state brought much prestige to the University.

In October 1977, Rusk was responsible for inviting Prince Charles, heir to the British throne, to visit the University and attend our football game against Kentucky.

It was a glorious occasion until the game started, when Kentucky proceeded to administer a sound licking to the home team. However, before the game, the prince, escorted by President Davison, received a rousing, royal Bulldog welcome. Fran Curci, the Kentucky coach, and I, with our respective captains, met the prince, and I gave him an autographed football from the team. Curci, in a startling gesture, extended his hospitality by unfolding the foil wrapper of a piece of gum, extending his hand, and loudly saying, "Gum, Prince?" I will never forget the expression on the stunned prince's face as he backed away, raising his open hands, shaking his head, and saying, "NO! NO!" I imagined the sophisticated prince must have thought to himself, "Another 'ugly' American."

Remarkably, all of these distinguished professors were highly productive throughout their long lives. Rusk died at eighty-four, Dodd at eighty-seven, Odum at eighty-eight, Giles at ninety-four, and Burton at ninety-five! All subscribed to the E. Merton Coulter theory of wearing out rather than rusting out! That theory, expressed in different words, would also apply to the remarkable J. W. Fanning, who in many ways should be mentioned in the same breath with these distinguished professors. Fanning was not a recipient of the bicentennial silver medallion nor did he achieve national or international fame, but his service to the University and the state surely parallels the careers of all those lifelong servants.

Fanning, a University graduate and later extensive service employee, became the first Vice President of Public Service ("Outreach" was added to the position title in 1997) during the Aderhold administration in 1965. When he retired in 1971, his service continued by becoming advisor-emeritus to Leadership Georgia. He developed the "ten pillars of leadership" that catapulted the Georgia program as one of the best state leadership programs in the country. Fanning died at ninety-two, living by his motto to stay "alive as long as you live," which became the title of Fanning's excellent biography written by his successor, S. Eugene "Gene" Younts, who actively served the state and the University with distinction for over thirty-one years.

Thanks primarily to newspaper entrepreneur and Board of Regent member Dink NeSmith, a lasting tribute to Fanning was established with the Fanning Institute. The institute has been highly successful by partnering with communities in addressing problems and advancing services and efficiency throughout the state.

I would be remiss not to mention Peter Albersheim, another superstar scientist recruited by Davison. Davison persuaded Albersheim, who had won numerous scientific awards, and his entire complex carbohydrate research team to move from the University of Colorado to Georgia. In 1985, Albersheim and his capable partner, Alan Darvill, founded the complex carbohydrate research center at the University that is now housed in a marvelous facility. Barbara and I have great memories of a ten-day hiking trip with Albersheim and his family. The journey led us to the Wind River mountain range in Wyoming where we fly-fished in the Alpine Lakes region. We also took other fly-fishing trips to Alaska and New Mexico with this preeminent scientist, exceptional individual, and good friend.

I had the great pleasure of knowing all of these remarkable and inspiring individuals. I was always amused that these world-renowned professors and public servants followed the fortunes of our football and athletic teams. I enjoyed being around all of them, but none more so than Dean Rusk, whose office was located in a small two-story building that had earlier been Philosophical and then Waddel Hall. Every time I visited Rusk in his office I came away with a special feeling that I had been enlightened tremendously by being around him. I was always amazed at his knowledge of the team. He always had a positive remark about my television show that aired on Sundays after each game. His observations on a wide range of subjects provided a rich experience for me with every visit. The Dean Rusk Hall, which houses the Dean Rusk Center for International Law and Policy, located in the Law Library, is named for the former secretary of state.

Davison: The Fan

Fred Davison loved the University and the Bulldog sports teams. He enjoyed talking about all the teams, mainly football, and wanted them all to succeed. As fellow Rotarians, we often traveled to nearby Jefferson, Georgia, to attend makeups, and while driving we talked football. He could not get enough. For many years he

President Fred Davison

Georgia's famous track people watched football games from outside the stadium until 1980.

and his wife, Dianne, would come by the house on Saturday evenings after home football games to mix and mingle with Barbara and me and the assistant coaches and their wives. There were no others there except a few key staff people. Davison enjoyed being with the exclusive Bulldog football coaching fraternity. It was a respite for him from the daily problems of running a large and growing University.

Prior to the start of home football games, he would perform his presidential duties of socializing with his invited guests and the president of the visiting team. But once the game started, the socializing was over. He was on the front row, cheering like the wildest Bulldog fan. The front row of the president's box was a great place to be a fan, but that was not the case with basketball games, where the whole section of Bulldog supporters was aware of his fanatical support. The Bulldog fans loved it when he would loudly protest calls by the officials, which he often did. Dianne obviously had enough after warning him several times that his actions were not becoming of the president of the University of Georgia. He finally considerably toned down some of his extreme antics, especially with the officials, but you could tell he was not enjoying the games as he once did.

Davison's genuine support from the top had a profound effect on our football program. During his first year, 1968, we won the Southeastern Conference Championship and went on to win four more (1976, 1980, 1981, and 1982) during his tenure. The 1980 team also won the National Championship, the year Herschel Walker was a freshman. Walker was the crown jewel of the best recruiting class in my twenty-five years as Georgia's head football coach. There were some talented performers in that class that became All-Americans: the late Jimmy Payne, Freddie Gilbert, and the amazing Terry Hoage. I often said about that year that we signed the most-sought-after player in the country in Walker and the least-sought-after player in Hoage. Both became consensus All-Americans, Herschel for three years and Hoage for two.

Georgia was the only Division IA (Bowl Championship today) school to offer Terry Hoage a scholarship. He was a brilliant student with a 3.85 grade point average in genetics. He loved the game and later played thirteen years of professional football. Today, he is using his biology background by growing grapes and making excellent wines in Paso Robles, California. His first wine, a terrific Shiraz, is called "The Hedge," in honor of the famous Chinese privet (Ligustrum sinense) hedge that has surrounded Sanford Stadium since its dedication in 1929. Hoage and his teammates accentuated the traditional saying of "we got 'em between the hedges" by winning twenty-five consecutive games in Sanford Stadium during the four years he played for the Bulldogs.

Herschel, from the small town of Wrightsville, was Georgia's second Heisman Trophy winner. His performance on the field and his persona off the field make him the most popular player in all of Georgia athletics. He is the most determined and self-disciplined athlete I

have ever coached or seen. He made the Olympic bobsled team in 1992, and at last count, he is undefeated in mixed martial arts. He might be the best-conditioned fifty-year-old athlete in the world.

There were many other great players in that talented class, and their four-year record of 43-4-1 was the best of any team in the nation at that time. Herschel left early for the pros in 1983, but even without him the team went 10-1-1, upsetting undefeated and number-two-ranked Texas in the 1983 Cotton Bowl. During that amazing run, we had thirty-seven consensus All-Southeastern Conference players, including Buck Belue and Lindsay Scott, who combined for the greatest play (a ninety-three-yard touchdown pass against Florida in 1980) in Georgia football history. There were three other consensus All-Americans during that four-year run: Scott Woerner and kickers Rex Robinson and Kevin Butler.

It was during that tremendous four-year run that the traditional battle cry of the Bulldog fans "How 'Bout Them Dawgs" reached its zenith. The saying received national attention in the early 1980s when the Bulldogs went to the Sugar Bowl three straight years with the National Championship on the line. Renowned collegiate supersportscaster and color analyst Keith Jackson, originally from Roopville, in Carroll County, Georgia, was the announcer for those three games, repeatedly remarked with his unique voice, "How 'Bout Them Dawgs!"

While the golden years of the early 1980s accentuated some Georgia traditions, it was the demise of another: the famous "track people." After the National Championship year in 1980, some twenty thousand seats were added in the east end zone, bringing Sanford Stadium's total capacity to over eighty-two thousand for the 1981 season. Closing in the end zone brought to an end the famous track people, a proud, fierce group of fans who for a decade had gathered on the railroad embankment to watch the football games. For the 1976 Alabama game, some fifteen thousand camped out on the embankment by 7:00 p.m. the night before the game. They loved the Bulldogs, and this proud but sometimes overly rowdy bunch was often featured on national television during the games. I will never forget that when plans were being made to close in the end zone, a group of track people came by my office bearing a peti-

Herschel Walker

tion signed by a thousand other track people, imploring me not to end one of Georgia's greatest traditions. I sympathized with them but told them how important it was to accommodate all of our many fans who had been unable to secure tickets and watch the Dawgs. I also assured them they would go down in history as the famous track people who had been able to watch and cheer for their beloved Bulldogs FREE! It was all part of the glory of the golden years of Georgia football.

Davison was "lovin' it," but earlier in the mid-

1970s there were some struggling times that stressed the fans, the president, and me. We posted records of 7-4 in both 1972 and 1973, and in 1974 we were 6-6, which caused a lot of unrest in the Bulldog Nation. To make matters worse, going into the next year (1975) I had only one year left on my contract. I went to Davison and told him it was not good for the Georgia program to enter a challenging season with one year left on the head coach's contract. The situation would provide the media with plenty of material to speculate whether

Right: Coach Erk Russell, defensive coordinator for the Junkyard Dawgs

the season or each game might determine if I would be the coach in the future. I told Davison that kind of atmosphere would be distracting to the team, staff, and fans. Besides, my overall record had been solid, and we had won two SEC championships. I asked him to seriously consider a contract extension, which would defuse the upcoming crisis. To Davison's credit, he took my advice and quieted all the speculation by adding three more years to my contract just before the season. That year (1975) the team, labeled the "Junkyard

Dawgs," responded by going 9-3 with a trip to the Cotton Bowl. The next year (1976) the team won ten games (we only played eleven games then) and won the SEC Championship. Those were great years for the students and fans as "the Godfather of Soul," the internationally acclaimed James Brown, attended several games, firing up the crowd by dancing and singing "Dooley's Junkyard Dawgs." He had produced the song on the spot in a studio after reading the lyrics written by radio host Happy Howard. Davison's action of extending my contract in the tough times drew high editorial praise throughout the country, and the performance of those teams the next two years made for some spirited times in Bulldog country with James Brown leading the way.

The Sea Grant College

As fun as those early years were in 1975 and 1976, nothing in Bulldog annals can top the feat of the 1980 National Championship year. Almost every person who was associated in any way with the University or who adopted the Bulldogs as "our team" felt a sense of pride in Georgia's being declared the undefeated, undisputed national champions and number-one football team in America.

Amid all the celebration in Athens and throughout the state that year, there was a much quieter but very meaningful celebration going on at the University when it was announced that year that Georgia was declared a National "Sea Grant" College. This recognition basically paralleled Georgia's being recognized as a National "Land Grant" College that took place over a hundred years earlier. The land grant funds that were made available to the University after the Civil War were a godsend to a very economically depressed institution. The federal funds that were available, for instance, enabled the College of Agriculture and Mechanical Arts to open in 1872.

Since the federal funds became available to the University through the sea grant designation in 1980, the institution has performed high quality research. While half of Georgia's sea grant funds have gone directly into scientific research on Georgia's coastal resources, the other half has gone toward communications, educational outreach, and administrative activities.

I had the privilege of visiting on various occasions both the Marine Institute in Sapelo as well as the Extension Station in Brunswick. On several occasions, while visiting the Brunswick Station in the 1980s, I took expeditions on the University's shrimp boat that had been converted to a research vessel. Named *The Georgia Bulldog*, the boat has been captained by Lindsey Parker for over thirty years. I recall how the Brunswick Extension Station was carrying out its mission of service by reaching out to the shrimping industry and helping it

with techniques and technology to become more productive. I also recall how the Bulldog research vessel helped the shrimpers bottom fish with long lines for the newly discovered golden tile fish found in twelve hundred feet of water. This venture enabled the shrimpers to be very productive in the off-season. The Federal Environmental Agency, however, in recent years has limited the deep-sea fishing catch, making the practice less productive for the shrimpers.

The other outreach program that is ongoing with the shrimpers concerns the development of the turtle exclusion devices on the shrimp nets to address the endangered sea turtle problem. In fact, one of the most effective turtle release devices was named in 1992 the "Parker TED" (turtle exclusion device) after *Bulldog* Captain Lindsey. The *Bulldog*, under Captain Lindsey, currently is developing an index of sea turtles to substantiate the effectiveness of the turtle exclusion devices, and the results so far have been very successful.

At the time of the visits to the research centers in the early 1980s I was both head football coach and athletic director, but having that dual responsibility was not without controversy.

Athletic Controversy and Prosperity

Joel Eaves, our athletic director, stepped down in 1978, and there was a huge controversy about who would be the next athletic director. At the time, the trend in intercollegiate athletics was to get away from the old tradition of having coaches take on the dual responsibilities of coaching and administration. I agreed with the theory, especially with the challenges of Title IX and expanding women's sports programs. However, I felt my situation was different. I had been an assistant athletic director to Eaves, and my seventeen years of experience at Georgia gave me an insight into what the program needed in the changing and challenging times of Title IX. Besides, I felt I had a broad perspective and a genuine desire to develop a total athletic program. Despite the concern of appearing overly ambitious, I felt that I was the best choice for Georgia at the time.

Davison had other ideas and wanted to appoint Forestry Professor Reid Parker, who served as faculty chair, as Athletic Director. A number of influential

Band and cheerleader from the Block *G* days

alumni and supporters did not agree with a faculty person being in charge of athletics and felt I would be the best choice. It was not a good situation and was getting worse by the day. Convinced this was a no-win situation for Davison and the University, I went to him and offered a compromise with the department's being run by dual athletic directors: myself as athletic director for sports programs and Parker as athletic director for administration. Davison liked the idea, and the decision eased the tension and resolved the issue for two years, until he named me full-time athletic director in 1981. I might add, winning the National Championship in 1980 and the offer by Auburn to return to my alma

mater didn't hurt his deciding that I had proved myself capable of doing both jobs.

My first job in 1979 as athletic director was to hire a full-time women's basketball coach for the chaotic program that had long been run by part-time coaches. The first hire turned out to be the ultrasuccessful Andy Landers, the first and only (thirty-four years as of 2011) full-time coach Georgia women's basketball ever had. At the top of the list of the many great women basketball players produced by Landers was Cairo, Georgia, native Teresa Edwards, a two-time consensus All-American. She became the most decorated Olympic basketball player in the world, participating in five

Dan Magill

Olympics, a feat never duplicated. Edwards and her best friend and another Landers All-American and Olympian, Katrina McClain, carried the 1996 Centennial Olympic torch together on campus, running past Stegeman Coliseum, where they played together.

At the same time, Coach Hugh Durham's teams were very successful in the early 1980s with superstar Dominique Wilkins, who later played for the Atlanta Hawks and became one of the all-time great professional basketball players. In 1983, the Georgia team (even without Wilkins) earned a trip to the Final Four. Tennis under Dan Magill, who built the program from scratch, went on to win two National Championships in 1985 and 1987. Magill produced many accomplished players, but perhaps the most celebrated was Mikael Pernfors, who won the 1987 NCAA singles championship while leading the team to the National Championship. In 2011, twenty-five years later, he was still on the pro circuit.

Our goal was to provide each of our sports programs with the facilities and finances to give our coaches a chance to compete for National Championships. That philosophy applied to all our sports.

Title IX and women's athletics, meanwhile, exploded on the scene at the University. I am proud to say that under the direction of the late Liz Murphey, we were out in front in women's sports in the country. In addition to being the associate athletic director for women's sports, Murphey was also the golf coach, and she was especially proud of Athenian Terri Moody, a terrific golfer who became one of our first female All-Americans.

I remember visiting with Murphey about Title IX even before women's athletics were absorbed into the NCAA in 1982. The Georgia women's program, which had been operating out of the physical education department, officially became part of the Athletic Association a few years earlier. I told Liz we did not really know what Title IX meant at the time, since there were controversial discussions going on nationally regarding interpretations. I told her that until these interpretations were finalized, we could set our own philosophy of doing what we perceived as being right. This meant women's teams should have the same support in scholarships, equipment, and facilities as comparable men's teams. Our definition proved to be not too far off (except for football), and this emphasis gave our women's program a big jump nationally. We hired, for the most part, excellent coaches, many of whom had extraordinary careers. They in turn recruited good student-athletes, and we provided good facilities for the teams. Our women's programs have enjoyed much success, winning numerous SEC and National Championships. We were fortunate that our football teams were having such great success at the time, because this enabled us to fund a large investment in our women's programs.

At the same time we were expanding our programs with the hiring of competent coaches, we were also expanding our staff to generate more revenue. One such example was the hiring of Avery McLean in 1981, the first full-time director of athletic promotions and marketing at the University and perhaps the first in intercollegiate athletics in the county. McLean, a University business school graduate, became a pioneer in sports administration studies by being one of

the first to receive a master's degree in the subject at Miami of Ohio. Since that time many schools have offered the program academically, including the University of Georgia.

After graduation, McLean secured a full-time job as promotion and marketing director of the NBA Utah Jazz. His first objective at Georgia in 1982 was to develop a licensing program that eventually produced millions in revenue. Today, the marketing revenue in Georgia athletics is over $4 million annually.

The most profitable licensing symbols at the time, which remain so today, are the Bulldog and the oval G marks. Many people have asked that I explain the origin of the oval G logo. There is a detailed history of the symbol in the annual football media guide under Georgia traditions. In essence, however, I chose to replace Georgia's block G with an oval forward-looking G in 1964, my first year as Georgia's head football coach. Ann Donaldson, a University art graduate, sketched out the oval G design. Her husband was our backfield coach, John Donaldson, a Georgia graduate who played with Charley Trippi in 1946. I had been impressed with Georgia's colors of red and black tempered with white. I had once read that the color combination of black on white on red are the most harmonious colors in existence. Applying the combination of the black oval G on a white decal to a red helmet made for a spectacular showing. To ensure there was no conflict with Green Bay's G, Coach Eaves called the Packers, informing them of our intentions.

As I look back, it was a radical departure from the silver headgear and the blocked G that only a naive young coach would attempt. Thanks to winning two Southeastern Conference Championships in the first five years, the change was well received. The oval G logo has withstood the test of time and remains one of the most important symbols and marks to the University and the licensing program.

While sports were flourishing at the University during the Davison era at Georgia, there were serious national problems, mostly caused by NCAA attempts to adjust to racial integration and well-intended attempts to provide opportunities to disadvantaged minority student-athletes. This resulted in drastically lowering academic qualifications for scholarships, which in turn brought Davison to the forefront as a national leader in sports.

Davison: A National Sports Leader

In the early 1970s, the NCAA had a reasonably good standard for scholarship eligibility based on a predictability formula of test scores, class rank, and grade point average known as the "1.6 rule." It worked well, and with tutoring help and hard work, graduation rates were fairly comparable to the student body at Georgia and most other institutions in the country.

Primarily because of the concerns of racial bias in test scores and possible lawsuits in that regard, the NCAA in the mid-1970s eliminated the reasonable 1.6 predictability standards, replacing it with practically no standard at all. The new requirement eliminated test scores and class rank. The only requirement was a high school diploma and a 2.0 grade point average in all high school subjects. This standard allowed practically all athletes graduating from any high school to be scholarship eligible. In order to compete, institutions were allowing coaches to recruit large numbers of high-risk student-athletes, subsequently causing graduation rates to plummet.

Meanwhile, Davison was elected president of the newly formed College Football Association (CFA), an organization of sixty-one institutions (the Big 10 and Pac 10 refused to join) around the country that would meet annually to develop a stronger voice in the NCAA. At that time, the NCAA rules allowed all schools, regardless of classification, to vote on all issues. The vast majority of the schools outvoted the larger football-playing institutions, and the CFA was a way to balance the ledger.

Another issue of great concern to the CFA was the NCAA total dominance of the television package. The NCAA controlled all appearances, to the detriment of many schools in the CFA. The University of Georgia and the University of Oklahoma took the initiative for the CFA and sued the NCAA. The question to be answered: was the NCAA in violation of the Sherman Antitrust Act? The judge found the NCAA was indeed in violation, calling the NCAA a "classic cartel." This action opened up sports television to what we have today.

Meanwhile, in the spring of 1982, Davison, working with CFA executive director Chuck Neinas, arranged a meeting of fourteen college sports leaders at the R. J. Reynolds plantation on Sapelo Island, Georgia, to discuss some of the ills of college athletics. Reynolds, the tobacco magnate and billionaire, had deeded most of his Sapelo property to the University to establish a marine research center during the Aderhold presidency. Among the invitees who stayed at the Reynolds mansion were noted presidents, athletic directors, and football and basketball coaches. These included presidents Fred Davison (Georgia), Bill Leavy (Virginia Tech), Jim Wharton (LSU), and Jim Zumberg (University of Southern California); athletic directors Homer Rice (Georgia Tech), Deloss Dodds (Texas), and me; and football coach Joe Paterno (Penn State) and basketball coach Bobby Knight (Indiana.)

The night before the conference officially started, an incident occurred during dinner that might have aborted the entire meeting. Southern California president Jim Zumberg and Indiana basketball coach Bobby Knight nearly came to blows over a dispute about Southern Cal's being put on serious NCAA probation at the time. I was sitting across from the two red-faced combatants as they shouted and stared at each other. Fortunately, we were able to separate the two before they came to blows.

The next morning we met and used a group round-chair format, with each person giving his thoughts on the problems in college athletics. While several issues were discussed, the majority agreed that the major problem was the low academic standards. Thus, out of that two-day conference, the so-called Sapelo Group passed a resolution asking for a return to higher academic standards for student-athletes that included test score requirements. The result was the NCAA's adopting Proposition 48, which restored a reasonable standard for scholarship. Prop 48 was the seed of gradually toughening eligibility rules by the NCAA with consideration later given to culturally biased test scores. Today, the standards include minimum core courses, satisfactory progress toward graduation, a minimum grade point average, and a test score sliding scale. There are also scholarship penalties if institutions fall below graduation standards. The leadership provided by Fred Davison in hosting this important meeting at Sapelo Island gained for him and the University wide praise from institutions around the country.

These were some of the best of times for Davison and the University. There were frustrations along the way, including student and faculty unrest and eventually the Jan Kemp episode, which became the worst of times.

Campus Unrest

When Davison became president, his timing was perfect with financial support from the state being at an all-time high. That was not the case in having to deal with a much more active and expressive faculty and student body. Like the rest of the campuses across the country, the late 1960s and early 1970s were a period of widespread campus unrest.

The first protest at Georgia occurred in April 1968, during Davison's first year on campus. Several hundred University students marched on campus and demanded equal rights for women. Among the demands were no dorm curfews and an alcohol policy compatible with state law. They wanted all regulations for women to be equal to men. With little response from the administration, some 300 students staged a sit-in in the academic building, spending the night. Old faithful Dean Tate spent the night with them. They did not leave the building until the following night, after the fire marshal warned them that their presence was a fire hazard. Davison and the administration took action to discipline the leaders and eventually imposed a year suspension on the main leader, who was president of the radical Students for a Democratic Society. The issue of equal rights for women eventually became moot when the University, like most institutions around the country, did away with its traditional role of surrogate parents (*in loco parentis*).

At the same time the campus was experiencing a more active student body, athletic coaches were experiencing a more expressive generation of student-athletes. While we never abandoned our role as surrogate parents with the athletes, we did lessen some of our strictest regulations and became conscious of treating them more as adults. It turned out to be a positive experience for the student-athletes, coaches, and administrators.

Meanwhile, on campuses around the country there were strong and even violent protests against the war in Vietnam. The most violent took place at Kent State University in Ohio, resulting in the tragic death of four students who were shot by a few overreactive members

Dean William Tate

of the Ohio National Guard who were sent to quell the rioting. The tragedy resulted in an uproar from students throughout the country.

At Georgia, a memorial service was held, and afterward a crowd of 4,000 marched to the president's house and then to the academic building, where Davison met with them at midnight to discuss the response to the tragedy by the University. The next day, the administration wisely decided to close the University for two days in memory of the dead Kent State students. While protests at Georgia were strong by a minority of students, historian Thomas Dyer felt the campus "never experienced the activism that characterized many other universities…and by the mid-1970s…the era of student protest and activism largely ended at the University."

While student protest ended on campus, student mischief moved to the forefront with the nude streaking fad. A large streaking jamboree of a few thousand took place one night on the campus in 1974, and there were several individual bare performances that surfaced in

Streakers from the 1970s

a variety of public gatherings. One of the more memorable was performed by a Vanderbilt student during a homecoming football game. Georgia dominated the game, but when a Vandy defensive tackle made a great tackle of the Georgia ball carrier, a Vanderbilt student discarded his raincoat and streaked onto the field wearing only some boots and hugged the Vandy defender for his tackle. The two teams stood dumbfounded as the streaker was pursued by campus security. It took the guards a while to corral and finally tackle this gifted broken-field runner, who by then had earned the support of a cheering crowd in the stands.

The Vandy streaker was looked upon as "good-natured madness," an appropriate phrase used by historian F. N. Boney to describe student foolishness. There were other acts of foolery, however, that went too far.

Peabody Hall

Unfortunately the longtime tradition of the homecoming senior parade around the football field at halftime had to be abandoned. It became a constant problem in the late 1960s and early 1970s as the senior class became larger and the celebration became more boisterous, obviously aided by too many libations. Its death knell came at halftime of the 1970 Ole Miss game when rowdy students paraded around the field with vulgar signs aimed at the opponent. Davison was infuriated, and the incident ended a great student tradition.

Faculty Unrest

While the students were publicly protesting on campus, a quiet controversy was brewing with the faculty over new guidelines instituted by Davison for promotion and tenure. The president declared that "promotion should be used as a tool to protect the University against incompetence in teaching, research and service." This did not sit well with many faculty members.

To make matters worse, Davison appointed Chemistry Department head S. W. Pelletier as provost to administer the controversial new guidelines. Pelletier was an intelligent, capable scientist, but he came across as a stern, "heavy-handed" administrator. Within a short period of time, the law school, the history department, and the journalism school all had bouts with Pelletier and his authoritarian style.

Once Pelletier and the promotion issue came into conflict with the journalism school, the controversy became public. An Atlanta newspaper called it a "brawl in academia." The controversy festered as the administration held firm with the promotion system and Pelletier's stern enforcement. The College of Arts and Sciences took up the charge, and in a faculty poll, Pelletier was strongly censured, and he was forced to resign shortly thereafter.

The position of provost was soon abolished and replaced by the Office of the Vice President for Academic Affairs. The first woman vice president in University history, Virginia Y. Trotter, a former Assistant Secretary of the U.S. Department of Health, Education, and Welfare, was appointed to the position.

Davison ended the decade of the 1970s with strong support from all the deans of the thirteen schools and colleges, except the dean of Arts and Sciences. The dean, who later resigned, represented a majority of the art and sciences faculty, considered the most liberal in the University. Most of the disagreement with the administration came from this group who bided their time until the president became vulnerable during the Jan Kemp crisis.

The Jan Kemp Crisis: The Worst of Times

The seeds of the Jan Kemp crisis were sown in the halls of the NCAA convention of the mid-1970s. The convention overreacted to the federal mandate that educational institutions had to make an effort to open their doors

Athens City Hall clock tower

to minority students who had, in the past, been denied access. As earlier discussed, the NCAA did so by voting out the reasonable 1.6 formula standard for initial scholarship eligibility and replacing it with a simple 2.0 high school average in any combination of courses upon graduation. To stay athletically competitive at the highest level, most institutions (including Georgia) recruited too many at-risk student-athletes who were not proficient in basic English and math. A Department of Developmental Studies was set up at the University under the direction of Dr. LeRoy Ervin. It was a good program at the time, and many students as well as student-athletes moved through the noncredit courses and into the mainstream of the University and graduated.

Jan Kemp had earned a degree in journalism and a doctorate in English education at UGA. She was a remedial English professor and apparently a good one. In some cases, less qualified students had to repeat some of the nonremedial courses two or three times before exiting. The University set up a system that after the third time of failure to exit into the University's regular courses, individuals could be administratively discharged by Vice President for Academic Affairs Virginia Trotter. When nine football players were administratively exited to the mainstream of the University's regular courses prior to the 1982 Sugar Bowl, the charge of preferential treatment for athletes gained national attention.

Prior to the lawsuit, Kemp had complained for some time about Dr. Ervin, the department head. Some of the complaints were justified. Ervin was even accused of having his own agenda. He apparently was helping not only student-athletes to enter and exit the system but also sons and daughters of influential people apparently for his own benefit, but in his mind to the benefit of the University.

This constant conflict with Kemp resulted in the University's dismissing her on the grounds of "disruptive conduct and for failure to conduct adequate scholarly research." She probably was guilty of both, but the combination of being stonewalled by the administration and then fired caused her to file suit at an opportune time. The administrative exit of the football players prior to the Sugar Bowl had drawn state and national attention.

Prior to the suit, she sent me a handwritten fifteen-page letter with a multitude of accusations. We met for an hour to discuss the complaints. I found that approximately 70 percent of the complaints had no merit. I told her I could not respond to the other complaints but assured her I would look into them. I found that about half of those complaints had no merit, but the other half were legitimate problems that needed to be addressed. I think Kemp always appreciated the fact that I took the time to visit with her.

In retrospect, I believe it was a bad mistake by the administration not to listen to her at some level beyond the developmental studies director. The other mistake obviously was going to trial. Some accused the administration of arrogance for that decision. Davison and his advisors sincerely believed they were right in dismissing her, and by winning the case, they would set precedents for dealing with future cases of disgruntled faculty members.

The case that came to trial in 1986, ironically with Federal Judge Horace Ward proceeding, was poorly defended and superbly prosecuted. The jury found in favor of Kemp and an award against the University of $2.6 million was later reduced to $1.1 million. The verdict set off a media frenzy as well as a political frenzy, resulting in the athletic program's being investigated with the utmost scrutiny. We were investigated by the Attorney General, the NCAA, the faculty, and on a daily basis by the media. The faculty investigation provided the opportunity for many Arts and Sciences professors who had deep-seated issues with Davison to vent. Meanwhile, we were being peppered from all sides.

We finally adopted the philosophy that we couldn't stand up every day and answer everything that was being thrown at us. We said that if the program was on solid ground, we would survive. We decided to treat the crisis as an opportunity to make the program better. We might be bruised or have a black eye, but we would survive and be better for it. That's exactly what we did, and that is exactly what happened. As part of our response to the crisis, we raised our academic standards higher than the rest of the SEC, which hurt us in the short term, especially when it came to signing big linemen. It hurt in some of those big games, as when we played Auburn, which played linemen we couldn't sign. But in the long run it helped us. Eventually the rest of the league adopted our standards.

We took further action by securing the services of retired Southeastern Conference Commissioner Dr. H. Boyd McWhorter, who formerly had been an UGA English teacher and later dean of the College of Arts and Sciences. McWhorter, a highly respected person by those in academia and athletics, became an athletic-academic consultant with an office in the Athletic Association, but he reported directly to the president. Another positive that came out of the crisis was that the athletic de-

The Dawgs run onto the field through the band in a pregame tradition.

partment became the first in the nation to develop a mission statement. We met with Cohn & Wolfe (a public relations firm), and they suggested putting together a statement of our principles and what our department stood for. It took us a year and a half to finalize what we wanted to say. Our mission statement program became a model for athletic programs around the country.

In the wake of the scandal, Kemp became either a hero or a villain, but Ervin was demoted and his pay was reduced. Trotter was reassigned to the College of Home Economics, but the saddest outcome of all was the resignation of President Davison.

I believe that if Davison had been more patient,

he would have survived the crisis. However, when the Board of Regents decided to delay his yearly appointment, Davison's pride was hurt (with good reason), and he resigned in a fit of anger. It was indeed the worst of times and ironic that Davison, who had transformed the school into a nationally ranked research institution, would be tarnished by a system that he was a leader in initially reforming. His initiative in putting together the Sapelo meeting was the beginning of reforming the flawed academic eligibility system that eventually caused his undoing. The entire episode was a burden for the University to bear for several years.

After his retirement, Davison became the successful president of the National Science Center in Augusta. All the while he maintained his interest in Georgia football. We set aside a small box in Sanford Stadium for him and his family. He was at almost every game, and I always saw and visited with him at the Georgia-Florida game in Jacksonville.

Prior to his death in 2004, the life sciences building that Davison had planned, promoted, secured state funding to build, and helped design was named in his honor. It was a fitting tribute to a president who served his University faithfully for nineteen years, making scientific research a top priority. Both Davison and his wife, Dianne, who died in 2005, are buried near the entrance of the Oconee Hill Cemetery across from his beloved University and the football stadium.

Dr. Henry King Stanford and the University of Georgia

When Davison retired, the Board of Regents turned to seventy-year-old Henry King Stanford, who possessed a wealth of presidential experience in higher education. Stanford had served as president for twenty-nine years at four different institutions, including his last nineteen as president of the University of Miami. He and his wife, Ruth, had retired to Americus, Georgia, living in the same historic antebellum Greek Revival cottage style house they had lived in while Stanford served as president of Georgia Southwestern College from 1948 to 1950.

I recall thinking, when I first heard the announcement, who is this Henry King Stanford, and how does he feel about athletics? Ironically, just a few days later, a short, bald-headed man introduced himself to me on the tram at the airport as Henry King Stanford! I was at first startled and then somewhat embarrassed that he introduced himself to me, but I thoroughly enjoyed this short visit with this energetic, jovial man whom I soon came to love and respect.

He was the ideal person to start the process of steering the University through the crisis and restoring morale on campus and throughout the state. He possessed the great attribute of having tremendous presidential experience combined with the fervor and enthusiasm of a college sophomore.

Stanford was an energetic optimist who was proud of the fact that he was traveling the state and "preaching the good news" about the University, as he would often say. He made 180 speeches to various groups across the state as the "institution's self-appointed evangelist."

On campus, he was a people's president, showing up unannounced at a variety of places and talking to students, staff, and faculty. An early indication of his presidential style was the way he traveled from Americus to Atlanta for the announcement of his appointment as interim president. I can still see the picture that appeared on the front page of the *Atlanta Journal-Constitution* of Henry King stepping off the Trailways bus at the Atlanta terminal on his way to the Regents office.

While traveling the state and preaching the "good news" about the University as a research institution, he cited several national surveys to back his claims. In 1986, the Carnegie Commission on Higher Education, as an example, ranked Georgia as one of the fifty-two leading research universities out of 2,800 colleges in the nation. Stanford also noted that the National Science Foundation ranked the University thirty-fourth the previous year (1985). He referred to the rankings as remarkable, "considering the absence of an engineering school and medical school from the flagship campus in the state."

Dr. Wesley Wicker, Vice President of University Advancement at Kennesaw State University, wrote his doctoral dissertation on Stanford. Wicker stated that despite Stanford's proclamation of the University's academic ranking and its academic integrity, "throughout the state the dominant issue with the public and the press seemed to center on the fate of the athletic program."

The Faculty Reform Committee composed of many professors of the College of Arts and Sciences who had a long-harbored resentment of President Fred Davison wanted the Athletic Association to cease to operate as a separate unit. While Stanford was willing to make adjustments in the structure of the athletic board to ensure more faculty involvement and control, he said, "I will not recommend the dissolution of the Athletic Association…and incorporate the $12 to $14 million debt of the Athletic Association into the University."

Stanford did reconstruct the athletic board so that

Terry College

instead of the president's appointing all faculty members, there would be three appointed by the president and three voted on by the University council. In addition to faculty members, the athletic board is composed of alumni and student representation. However, by design to ensure institutional control, faculty members always outnumbered alumni board members.

Stanford also endorsed my recommendation that Dr. Boyd McWhorter, former Southeastern Conference Commissioner and former Dean of the College of Arts and Sciences, be appointed as an academic consultant who reported directly to the president on the academic progress of the student-athletes. The president wanted to assure the faculty that "the Athletic Association... would have no decision-making role in the academic affairs of the University" and that "absolute authority over all academic matters resides...in the academic offices and with faculty members of the University." All

of the faculty members were pleased, of course, with the raising of academic requirements for athletes that Stanford supported.

While tempering the more radical faculty about athletics, Stanford had to address the feelings and morale of the Bulldog Nation around the state. Some of the more rabid football followers saw Stanford as crippling football and turning the University into the "Harvard of the South." Longtime popular Bulldog sportscaster Larry Munson, a folk hero to the Bulldog Nation, repeatedly stated on the radio, "Stanford's leaning toward academics has dropped Georgia into a league with the Vanderbilts, Rices, and Northwesterns of the world!"

An unrattled and confident Stanford quipped that "reducing the University to another Vanderbilt sounded like a real compliment." However, he went on to say that "college sports pose dangers of excess, but they generate enthusiasm...that spills into support for academic programs sometimes." To prove his point, two of the University's most generous financial contributors to academics at the University—Bernard Ramsey and Herman Terry—can trace the origin of their support to athletics.

The ability to balance both sides of the controversy and to keep the lids on many pots from boiling over is a tribute to Stanford's wealth of experience, his unselfish attitude, and his excellent leadership qualities. Long-time respected University English professor George Marshall, chair of the ad hoc Committee on Policies during those turbulent times, said, "Stanford's greatest contribution was the present climate of respectful differences of opinion."

Just as Stanford was implementing change and moving toward healing a very wounded University, the announcement was made that the search committee had found a full-time president. The committee was chaired by Tom Cousins, a highly respected University alumnus and real estate mogul and philanthropist. Cousins and his committee recommended and the Regents approved Dr. Charles "Chuck" Knapp, Senior Vice President of Tulane University, as the next president. At the very moment the announcement was made, the take-charge interim president Henry King halted being a highly active president and delayed decisions on all issues to the incoming president.

While I was happy that a permanent president would now be running the University, I was saddened that the best year I ever enjoyed under any president would be coming to an end. Stanford had guided the University through some turbulent waters, and there were signs that the healing process was well on its way. I personally had hoped that he would stay around for another four years to "finish the drill," a phrase later coined by football coach Mark Richt.

After Stanford returned to Americus, he maintained his relationship with his many new friends at the University. I was fortunate to be one of them who was able to continue enjoying the wit and wisdom of this remarkable man, described as "a classic scholar, a moral example, and authoritative figure" to thousands of students.

Each year that I would return to Albany to speak to the annual Southwest Georgia Bulldog Rally, Dee Matthews, the lifetime president of the club, always made sure that Henry King was an honored guest. He relished the occasion and always dressed in his finest Bulldog regalia, sporting the red shoes he claimed I gave him. He would entertain and inspire the Bulldog faithful with his splendid oratory.

Always active, Dr. Stanford returned to the University often, appearing at times in the strangest places at the strangest times. During a home football game in my last year of coaching in 1988, Henry King spontaneously appeared next to me on the sidelines during the heat of the battle to say hello. After initially recovering from the shock, I thanked him for dropping by and politely excused myself to return to the "coaching chaos" of the sidelines. His surprise appearance was vintage Henry King!

Even as his health faded after turning ninety years old and he was assigned to an assisted living home, he never lost his energy or enthusiasm. The last time I saw him in the nursing home we took a picture together (with him in a Bulldog football jersey) that he used as a Christmas card.

Stanford passed away at ninety-two on New Year's Day 2009, and like some of the other giants of the University, he never "rusted out" and "lived as long as he was alive." He left all who knew him with very special memories. The most favorite and the most lasting for me was the quote he often used from Alfred Lord Tennyson's *Ulysses*: "I am part of all I have met." Being a small part of the Henry King Stanford era rates at the top "of all I have met."

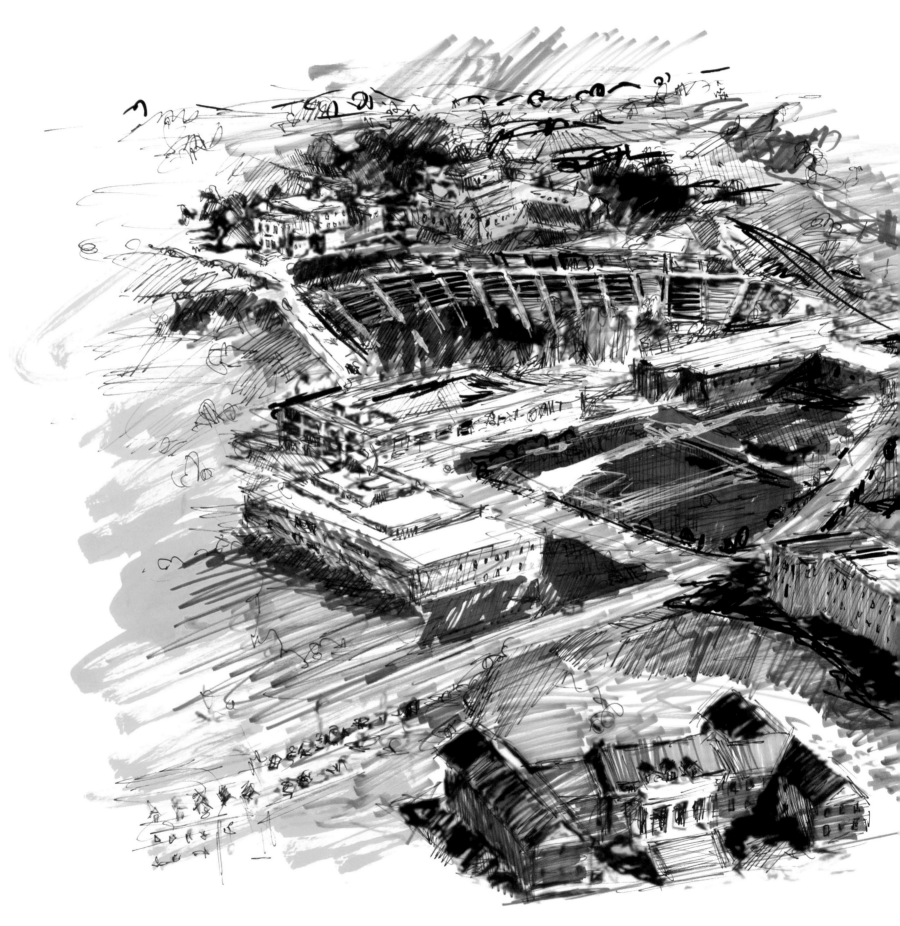

University of Georgia campus on Ag Hill

$\mathcal{M}$ODERN ERA

President Charles B. "Chuck" Knapp

In the summer of 1987 Dr. Charles B. "Chuck" Knapp became the twentieth president of the University of Georgia. He brought to the University an excellent background balanced with experience in teaching, administration, and government service. A native of Ames, Iowa, Knapp received his bachelor's from Iowa State and his master's and PhD in economics from Wisconsin in 1972. He taught economics at Texas for four years and was later summoned to Washington, D.C., as part of the Carter administration, eventually serving as Deputy Assistant Secretary of Labor until 1981. After a year at George Washington University as Associate Professor of Public Policy, he was hired at Tulane University and taught economics and served as Senior Executive Vice President. It was in that capacity that he became directly involved in intercollegiate athletics for the first time. It was a tragic experience, and the episode got my attention when it was announced he would be our new president.

In 1985, Tulane's men's basketball program became involved in one of the biggest scandals in college athletics. Four players were accused of shaving points in games for money and cocaine. Knapp, in his capacity as executive vice president, was directly responsible for addressing the scandal. As a result, the Tulane men's basketball program was abolished, and it was four years before the school resumed playing in 1988. Thus when Knapp came to Georgia, I was naturally suspicious of a president whose only direct experience in intercollegiate athletics was a scandal of the highest order that led to the disbanding of the program.

At the same time, Knapp had every reason to be suspicious of the athletic program he inherited at Georgia. As it turned out, both of our suspicions proved to be wrong. I found Chuck Knapp to be a man of integrity, trustworthy, and highly principled. This brings to mind a leadership class he was teaching at Georgia after his retirement. The subject was how to release a controversial decision to the public. He said that tough decisions should be made on principles first and only later presented in the best possible light. This told me a lot about Chuck Knapp. He was basically a low-key person, unassuming, and willing to listen. Once he became confident of the leadership of our athletic program, he was a great supporter.

President Knapp admitted to me later that, given the Jan Kemp scandal, he was naturally suspicious of the athletic program when he arrived. However, as he got to know me and learned how the program was run, he no longer had those reservations. He felt the program was run efficiently and with integrity. I was able to work with him as well as any president we've had at Georgia in my time. I met with him on a regular basis, just as I had with Presidents Davison and Stanford. Because of the high visibility of athletics, open dialogue between the athletic director and the University president is extremely important, and Knapp felt these regular meetings were of great benefit to him.

When Knapp arrived, his main mission was to "reestablish confidence in the academic reputation of the University." Interim President Henry King Stanford laid a solid foundation in restoring academic confidence in the University's reputation by diligently preaching the "good news" of the University as a research institution. Stanford also paved the way for Knapp by appointing beloved and highly respected Dr. Louise McBee as Interim Vice President for Academic Affairs. McBee, who served twenty-five years as a University administrator,

provided valuable assistance to Knapp in his first year of "learning the ropes" around the campus. She later served fourteen years as a state representative from Athens, and she was an advocate for the University and higher education. Working closely with Dr. McBee at the time was nationally recognized history scholar Dr. Thomas Dyer, who was Associate Vice President for Academic Affairs. Both worked as a team during the Kemp crisis and provided great help and counsel for us during our tribulations.

Among other steps we took to address the Jan Kemp crisis in 1986 was to hire Dick Bestwick, a longtime respected football coach and athletic administrator. Bestwick assumed a new position, Assistant Athletic Director for Student-Athlete Services. His main charge was to reach out and reestablish relationships with the faculty. Bestwick worked mainly with Dyer on academic matters involving student athletes. Dyer had attended the University of Missouri as an undergraduate and was a manager for the football team under hall of fame coach Dan Devine. He worked well with Bestwick, who also had ties to Missouri, once serving as an assistant athletic director for the Tigers.

Bestwick convinced me to convert the lounge area in McWhorter Hall, the athletic dormitory, into a student-athlete study and counseling area. While Bestwick concentrated on the men's academic issues, Glada Gunnels Horvat, who came up through the ranks as an UGA student, tutor, and counselor, headed up the women's academic effort.

That meager start as a facility in 1986 grew to a $7.5 million tutoring and high tech facility in 2002 known as the Rankin M. Smith Sr. Student-Athlete Achievement Center. The building is across from Stegeman Coliseum and the football practice fields. The site was once a navy preflight athletic facility, and after the war, it became the football team's field house under Coach Wally Butts. It was later converted to the University Alumni House before it was demolished to make room for the current Smith center. The facility is named in honor and memory of Rankin M. Smith Sr., a University alumnus, businessman, philanthropist, and longtime owner of the Atlanta Falcons football team. The funds were made available through the generosity of three of Smith's children: Taylor, Rankin Jr., and Dorothy Ann (Wa Wa) Hines.

A Bulldog Controversy

In addition to receiving positive reports from McBee and Dyer regarding the progress made academically with Georgia's student-athletes, Knapp received further reinforcement from his chief of staff, David Coker. Bestwick and Coker worked well together. Bestwick often told me that Coker was one of Knapp's best hires.

While Coker was a top hire by Knapp, the same could not be said of Nick Edes, a friend whom Knapp met and worked with while serving in the Labor Department in Washington. Edes was smart, crafty, and eager to take on tough situations. While in the Labor Department, Edes was often called a shark in getting things done. Some say Knapp felt he needed that personality type at Georgia while others contend Knapp owed Edes a favor. Whatever the reason for hiring Edes, it turned out not to be a good choice.

Edes, from Chicago, was for the most part not well received in Georgia. His signature dress was a sweater for most all occasions, and his demeanor was less than tactful. What got him into hot water was his attempt to standardize University stationery by using the Arch logo. As it turned out, this was a good idea. The stationery is still standard for the University. The problem came when some coaches and athletic department heads, who had been using a Bulldog logo on their stationery for recruiting purposes, thought they would have to change the Bulldog symbol to the Arch on their stationery. The word quickly (but unfairly) went around the state and eventually to the State Capitol that Edes was trying to get rid of the Bulldog as Georgia's mascot. Edes was a bright and very interesting person, and I got along well with him, but he came across as a rude northerner who wanted to get rid of the Bulldog as a mascot. That perception did not sit well around the state. Apparently, encouraged to leave, Edes resigned and headed to California, but he has kept his contact with Knapp and some friends at the University.

The HOPE Scholarship and the Eastward Expansion

A major part of Knapp's legacy is his upgrading of the University's academic reputation. This worthy accomplishment was supplemented by the extensive building program on what became the East Campus. Knapp was a respected academician with an effective consensus-building leadership style. He was also seen as a liberal Democrat. All of these qualities sat well with the majority of the faculty. He was also popular with many supporters in the Atlanta area but generally not as highly regarded by a more conservative south Georgia.

Nevertheless, Knapp worked extremely well with Georgia alumnus Zell Miller (BA 1957, MA 1958) who had spent almost a lifetime in politics. Miller rose from Lieutenant Governor to Governor (later U.S. Senator) and served the state as such from 1991 to 1999, during most of Knapp's tenure. Miller ran in 1990 on a bold ticket (at the time) that supported a lottery for higher education and won the approval from a majority of the Georgia voters. With the counsel of Knapp and other educators, the Miller experiment turned into the HOPE scholarship program, providing funds for tuition and books for those students in the state with a B average who attended Georgia's public schools.

The program was a bonanza for higher education. Many of the top students in Georgia, who in the past had left the state to go to North Carolina, Virginia, and other prestigious state and private schools, were now staying home. This pushed the academic reputation of the University to the next tier, and today it is regarded as one of the top public institutions in the country. It has been a two-edged sword, however, as many highly qualified students fell short of the exceedingly high academic standards for admission and many lost their HOPE scholarships when their grade averages fall below the required B average.

Meanwhile, Knapp went about his eastward expansion of the campus. The biggest and most expensive project was the much-needed student physical activities building, which became known as the Ramsey Center in memory of the late wife of the University's most generous donor, Bernard Ramsey. A Macon product and 1937 University graduate, Ramsey made his fortune in New York with Merrill Lynch, maintaining his connection with the University through his longtime friend and classmate Bill Hartman, who was also an All-American football player. Ramsey often returned for football games in those years, which kept him in touch with the University.

PENLEY

Billy Payne

Funding for the $40 million building came primarily through student fees, although the Athletic Association pledged $7.8 million for using the building for volleyball, swimming and diving, gymnastics, and basketball. The Association put up front $2.8 million of the $7.8 million to finance design and preparation costs. This type of financing was another example of the benefit of the separately incorporated Athletic Association.

The 430,000-square-foot Ramsey Center for Physical Activities provides three swimming pools in the huge Gabrielson Natatorium, five gymnasiums, a large workout facility, an indoor track, a climbing wall, and numerous handball courts. The complex, when first completed, was the best facility of its kind in the country, and today it remains one of the best in the nation. Close by the Ramsey Center is the Cultural Center of the University, another tangible sign of Knapp's leadership. The area contains the performing and visual arts complex that includes the Georgia Museum of Art, the Performing Arts Center, the Hugh Hodgson School of

Music, and the Lamar Dodd School of Art.

The entire area was completed just in time for the 1996 Centennial Olympic Games, during which the University hosted three Olympic events, opening its campus doors to the world.

Billy Payne: The Olympics Come to the University

William Porter "Billy" Payne, a University "Double Dawg" graduate (AB 1969, JD 1973), and his 1996 Centennial Olympic team pulled off one of the most amazing accomplishments in the state and perhaps the nation by bringing the Olympics to Atlanta against overwhelming odds.

Payne was born in Athens, where his father, Porter Payne, was attending the University and playing football in the late 1940s for Coach Wally Butts. Billy Payne was part of the great Bulldog recruiting class of 1965 (my second year as head football coach) that featured such superstars as All-Americans and hall of famers Bill Stanfield and Jake Scott. That class formed the backbone of two Southeastern Conference Championships in 1966 and 1968. Payne, one of the best "sixty-minute players" I ever coached, was a consensus All-Conference selection in 1968 and was recognized by the Associated Press as Third Team All-American. He was also a national scholar-athlete honoree and vice president of the student body at the University. He helped coach our freshman team while he attended law school. Payne loved his experience at the University, and that affection for his alma mater was an important factor in the University's hosting three Olympic events.

Payne shared his improbable Olympic dream with me in 1990. Thinking of all the odds against it happening, I recall saying to myself, "Billy, those old licks you received in football have caught up with you!" It was a daunting challenge, to say the least, considering Atlanta was not well known internationally at the time. In addition, Los Angeles had just hosted the Olympic Games in 1984, and the Olympic Committee almost never awards the bid to the same country that soon. Besides, 1996 was the centennial year of the Olympics, and Athens, Greece, where it all started, would surely be chosen as the host city. Finally, to top it off, the seem-

ingly impossible task was the fact that no city in the one-hundred-year history of the modern Olympics had ever won the games on its first bid!

Sharing that dream with me was one thing, but sharing it with sponsors was another. They politely told him "no," thinking he was crazy. Thanks to several of his close friends who put up $10,000 each, Atlanta upset Minneapolis for the right to represent the United States in Tokyo, Japan, as one of the world's five bid cities.

I was determined to go to Tokyo for the event. As it turned out, President Knapp authorized me to represent the University during the selection process. The episode turned out to be one of the most tense and emotional moments of my life. I sat next to Billy's family, wife Martha, son Porter, and daughter Elizabeth (who was a student at the University). Elizabeth grabbed my hand and squeezed it as the International Olympic Committee chairman from Spain, Juan Antonio Samaranch, opened the envelope and in a Catalan voice announced, "The winner of the 1996 Summer Olympics is ATLANTA!" As I hugged Elizabeth, Porter, Martha, and finally Billy, I got so emotional that tears came to my eyes. I was exceedingly happy and proud for Atlanta, the state of Georgia, and the University, but most of all, as a coach, I was proud and happy for one of my favorite players in his greatest moment of glory. It was a terrific night of celebration for Billy, his family, his friends, and all the Georgia delegation who made the trip to Tokyo.

When I saw Billy the next morning, I reminded him not to "forget your alma mater." He smiled and said, "Don't worry." He was soon in a position to include the University as he became the first person in history of the Olympics to both lead the bid effort and to serve as CEO of the games themselves.

The University secured the medal round of one of the premier Olympic events, which I had lobbied for: men's and women's soccer. But also awarded to the University and Athens were rhythmic gymnastics and later (after a disagreement with Cobb County) the preliminaries of volleyball. Soccer would be played in Sanford Stadium, and rhythmic gymnastics and volleyball would be hosted in Stegeman Coliseum.

I had a public relations issue converting Sanford Stadium to a soccer field, which required removing the

Stegeman Coliseum

hedges. Many football purists were not happy about removing "the sacred hedges" to play "soccer" in Sanford Stadium, not to mention playing "women's soccer." However, they were eventually satisfied when I let it be known that removing the Chinese ligustrum hedges was a blessing in disguise. A plant science team led by our faculty athletics representative, William "Bill" Powell, had discovered that the sixty-seven-year-old hedges had "nematodes," a potentially life-threatening disease. To further satisfy the skeptical football purists, we took cuttings from the original hedges and grew them at Dudley Nurseries in Thomson, Georgia, and at Hackney Nursery in Quincy, Florida.

Owners of both nurseries were Georgia graduates with strong University ties. Following the conclusion of the Olympics and with the first football game just three weeks away, we replaced the original hedge with its "sons and daughters." This new generation of hedges became known as "Hedges II."

The University Olympic experience was "par excellence." Stegeman Coliseum was draped in Olympic regalia and appeared stately and festive. Outside, the walkways were lined with large pots of colorful flowers. Sanford Stadium was also colorful and festive. The University Olympic experience was in sharp contrast to Atlanta. While there were open spaces on the campus for visitors to leisurely stroll after events, the masses in Atlanta were often herded through a crowded shopping area where they were "hawked" by an overkill of commercial vendors. While the Atlanta crowds often rushed to get to their hotel or home after the events, the crowds in Athens, much like a European city, strolled and enjoyed the ambiance of the day and the beauty of the campus. The assistant head of the World Volleyball Federation who was assigned to Athens for the preliminaries was initially not happy being in the Classic City as opposed to the big city of Atlanta. He later told me privately and then spoke publicly on the last day of the event in Athens that he "first thought he was being sent to purgatory, but I soon found out I was sent to heaven."

Seth Bladder from Switzerland, the deputy assistant to the World Soccer Federation who today heads that powerful organization, was exceedingly happy with the medal game experience at the University. I recall that when he toured the stadium, he was astonished that the facility was only used seven or eight times a year,

Broad Street

six or seven times for football and once for graduation! Internationally, stadiums are in constant use for soccer and other events. Bladder was also impressed with how well the events flowed at the University and the Classic City.

Dr. Knapp had assigned certain key people to co-ordinate the University's and community's involvement. Among the most notable were community leader Dink NeSmith, who chaired the Athens–University Olympic Committee, and Dr. Richard "Dick" Hudson, University administrator and faculty member who coordinated the University's involvement. Event manager Bill Knight, who once worked in the athletic department and later for World Cup Soccer, coordinated the events and fa-cilities. Bladder was amazed at how smoothly the event operations took place. He was not aware the Univer-sity community was well experienced in handling big crowds on football weekends.

Incidentally, the town-gown relationship was never better in this cooperative effort to show off the city of Athens and the University of Georgia to the world. In addition to the millions who saw Athens and the Uni-versity on television, there were some 650,000 visitors who came to UGA and the Classic City. Olympic record soccer (football) crowds saw Nigeria beat Spain for the men's gold medal and the United States beat China for the women's gold. The most spectacular moment of all the University Olympics occurred when the U.S. wom-en's soccer team paraded around Sanford Stadium with the American flag in a victory celebration.

Billy Payne made several trips back and forth to the University for Olympic events, but his most memo-rable trip was when he ran in the torch relay. Payne called me, announcing his plan to run the torch with his son Porter and daughter Elizabeth through the stadi-um, pausing at the fifty-yard line to honor his dad. He then wanted to pass the flame to me in the end zone. I was proud that Billy had involved his ole coach in such a momentous occasion. I might add, after Billy paused to light my torch, the Olympic official rerouted me *up* the steps to the bridge and *up* Sanford Drive and then *up* Baldwin Street before finally passing the flame to Dr. Knapp, who carried it through the campus. I will have to admit a cheering crowd helped get my adrenaline flowing to survive the endurance test *up* the steps and *up* the hills before gladly "passing the flame."

The aftermath of the 1996 Olympics saw the city and campus adorned with stately permanent works of art as reminders of the Centennial experience. In front of the Classic Center in downtown Athens stands a marvelous statue of the Greek goddess Athena, and en-graved on the statue's pedestal are the words from the Athenian Oath. In front of Stegeman Coliseum stands a fitting tribute to the Centennial Olympics by retired art professor John D. Kehoe of the University Studies Abroad "Cortona, Italy" fame. Jack, a former athlet-ic board member, sold me on the idea of the massive marble structure as a permanent Centennial Olympic memorial. It displays the five universal passions: awe, anguish, love, triumph, and joy, inscribed in seven of the leading languages of the world. Carved on the back of the structure is an ongoing record of all the Univer-sity of Georgia students who participated in the Olym-pics, starting in 1936 with world record holder Forrest "Spec" Towns. Included among the participants is Her-schel Walker of the 1992 bobsled team that competed in Alberville, France. As of this writing, there are 115 University of Georgia Olympic athletes inscribed on the back wall. Just above the names is a quote from Bil-ly Payne: "Through their talents, dedication and spirit they have brought glory to the University, the state of Georgia, their country and themselves,"

Payne's Olympic torch that was carried through the stadium in memory of his father is today encased facing the field in the main entrance in the southwest corner of the stadium. Payne brought great glory to ole Georgia with the Centennial Olympics and brought further glo-ry to his alma mater when in May 2006 he was named chairman of the Augusta National Golf Club. Working with Payne at the home of the world famous Masters golf tournament in Augusta is Will Jones, director of business affairs and University of Georgia graduate (BBA 1988) who played for me from 1984 to 1987. Payne has received many awards, but none is more special to him than being recognized by the National Collegiate Athletic Association (NCAA) in 1997 with its highest honor—the Theodore Roosevelt Award—as well as the Distinguished American Award in 2009 by the National Football Foundation and College Hall of Fame. He was also chosen in 2011 for induction in the prestigious UGA Circle of Honor, with the induction ceremony scheduled for 2012. These awards are extra special to Payne because they connect him directly to the experience at his alma mater and to his beloved Bulldogs, which he continues to follow today with great passion.

Change and Championships

Despite the positives we gleaned from the Jan Kemp incident, the crisis did affect football recruiting. Not being able to take some big linemen who were at risk academically was a factor in the downturn following the golden years from 1980 to 1983. We had mediocre records of seven wins both in 1984 and 1985 and eight wins in 1986. Despite the fact that the teams were good enough to play in bowl games each year, their records were below the high standards set in the early 1980s. In my last two years (1987–88) the teams were much more competitive, winning nine games each during eleven-game seasons and coming very close to winning another SEC championship.

It was during that time I seriously considered running for public office. I was completing my twenty-fifth year and had accomplished everything I had wanted to achieve as a football coach. At the same time, I thought the timing was right to pursue politics, an interest I had acquired through my study of history. I sincerely felt, and still do, that there is a need for good leadership in public service, and I came very close to jumping into the political arena. I had earlier thought about a run for the U.S. Senate, and now I thought about running for Governor. Mentally, I felt great about running for office, but never felt completely committed to the game of politics. In essence I lacked "the fire in the belly," a phrase considered essential in running for public office. Consequently, I decided against the idea and remained in athletics with the challenge of building a total athletic program.

Before I made the decision to stay in athletics, I actually retired from coaching and administration prior to the end of the 1988 season to contemplate running for Governor. I recommended to President Knapp that Erk Russell, who had been with me for seventeen years at Georgia before building an ultrasuccessful football program from scratch at Georgia Southern, would be the best person to succeed me as coach. I have no doubt Erk would have been highly successful for five, ten, or

any number of years he chose to coach at Georgia. It would have been a smooth transition and one popular with the Georgia people. It was obvious, however, that President Knapp had other ideas, and after a token attempt to recruit Erk, Knapp offered the job to a much younger Dick Sheridan, an excellent coach at North Carolina State. After Sheridan reluctantly turned the job down, Ray Goff became the leading contender.

Goff, an All-SEC quarterback from Moultrie, Georgia, had led our team to the Southeastern Conference Championship in 1976, and he was named the SEC's Most Valuable Player. After he had coached at South Carolina, I brought him back to the University as backfield coach and recruiting coordinator in 1981. Goff was an excellent recruiter and very popular with the Georgia people. He was personable, considerate, and being a "Georgia boy," he was the overwhelming choice of the people. I had some reservations about Goff since he was only thirty-three at the time. However, my good friend and longtime confidant, Georgia part-time assistant coach and successful Athens businessman Bill Hartman, believed that Goff would be the best choice. Hartman reminded me that I was only thirty-one when I first came to Georgia. I had the highest respect for Hartman, who as a University and community leader had done more for the institution over a long period of time that any other person I had known. Consequently, I was supportive of his opinion that Goff would be the best choice to succeed me.

Goff coached for seven seasons, had a good record of 46-34-1, and beat our rival Georgia Tech the last five years in a row. The highlight of his career was the 1992 team that went 10-2 and just missed winning the SEC Championship. Led by All-American running back Garrison Hearst and All-American quarterback Eric Zeier, the team beat Ohio State in the Citrus Bowl. The next three years, however, were not as good. His teams went 5-6, 6-4-1, and 6-6, losing to Tennessee and Florida three years in a row and Auburn twice. It was a very tough decision, but I decided to make a change.

My choice of Glen Mason had a poor result. He accepted the job but a week later decided to stay at Kansas after a child custody dispute with his former wife. I quickly hired Jim Donnan, who had been a highly successful head coach at Marshall University (64-21 in six seasons, a Division I-AA school at the time). He

PENLEY

Coach Manuel Diaz

Championships Galore

Meanwhile, our other sports teams were winning numerous championships, propelling our total program into one of the best in the nation. We hired some talented coaches, and they had developed highly successful teams over a period of time.

Manuel Diaz played and coached for the legendary tennis coach Dan Magill, and he succeeded him in 1988. Magill, who became the winningest tennis coach in NCAA history, had won the National Championship in 1985 and 1987. He won an astounding fourteen SEC Championships before turning over the reins to Diaz in 1988. As of this writing, Diaz has won four NCAA National Outdoor Championships in 1999, 2001, 2007, and 2008 and two National Indoor Championships in 2006 and 2007. He also has won an amazing thirteen SEC titles. Among the most noted stars to play for Diaz is six-foot-nine John Isner, who, during the course of a successful pro career, won the longest match in Wimbledon history. The match lasted eleven hours and five minutes over a three-day period. The score of the fifth and final set was 70–68.

Chris Haack took over men's golf in 1996 after a highly successful run by Dick Copas, who won seven SEC Championships. Haack so far has won two National Championships in 1999 and 2005 and seven SEC titles. His 2011 team finished second in the nation.

In baseball, Steve Webber took the team to its first College World Series in 1987 and won Georgia's only National Championship in 1990 but soon fell on hard times. Legendary Mississippi State baseball coach Ron Polk, who came out of retirement to coach Georgia for a couple of years, won the SEC Championship in 2001. Polk's assistant coach, David Perno, a former Georgia baseball player and native Athenian, succeeded Polk. He led the team to two SEC Championships, three trips to the College World Series, and in 2008 reached the National Championship game.

Women's sports produced even more championships at both the national and conference level. Jack Bauerle, a former Georgia swimmer and assistant coach, took over the women's program in 1979 and the men's program in 1983. While his men's teams have consistently been ranked in the top ten nationally most every year, it is the women's program that has pro-

was later inducted into the College Football Foundation Divisional Hall of Fame. Donnan gave us some great moments but eventually clashed with President Mike Adams in an incident to be discussed later. Like Goff, Donnan did not produce an SEC Championship team but did win four straight bowl games. We went a long twenty years after the SEC Championship of 1982 before we had another championship team.

I hired Mark Richt in December 2000, and in 2002 his team won the first championship in two decades that helped seal my image as a successful athletic director to the Bulldog populace. Regardless of the success of the entire athletic program, an athletic director is measured by the success of the football team.

Coach David Perno

duced championships. The women's swimming and diving team won the National Championship in 1999, 2000, 2001, and 2005. Bauerle has thus far won seven SEC Championships. The women's swim team has also produced a remarkable array of scholar-athletes and Olympians. The most remarkable achievement is that three of Bauerle's swimmers have been named NCAA Woman of the Year: Lisa Coole (tragically killed in a car accident), Kristy Kowal, and Kim Black. There is no institution in the country that has produced as many NCAA Woman of the Year recipients as Georgia, let alone all in one sport. Two of Georgia's most remarkable swimmers were All-Americans Courtney Shealy and Kristy Kowal, who won gold and silver medals, respectively, in the 2000 Olympics. Both were selected for the UGA Athletic Association's prestigious Circle of Honor, to be inducted in 2012 with Billy Payne.

The success of the women's gymnastics program under Suzanne Yoculan is even more amazing. Yoculan was not only a great coach who put together a su-

perb staff but was one of the best promoters I have seen in intercollegiate athletics. Her teams won National Championships in 1987, 1989, 1998, 1999, 2003, 2005, 2006, 2007, 2008, and 2009. Her teams also won an astounding sixteen SEC Championships. With no disrespect to this incredible achievement but rather to put in perspective the challenge of other sports, there is a big difference in the number of institutions competing nationally and in the SEC in the sport of gymnastics as compared to other sports. There are, for instance, only 63 gymnastics teams in the country and 7 in the SEC, compared to 194 women's swimming and diving teams nationally and 10 in the conference. In women's tennis there are 314 teams that compete nationally and 12 in the SEC. Likewise, there are 249 teams nationally and 12 in the SEC participating in women's golf. In women's basketball there are 335 teams that compete nationally and 12 in the SEC, and 283 in women's softball and 12 in the SEC.

The number of sensational gymnasts Yoculan has

Coach Jack Bauerle

the Honda Inspiration Award in 1992. A lot of credit for her amazing comeback should be given to her then boyfriend (now husband), Bulldog linebacker (1986-89) Matt McCormick, who became her personal trainer and attended all her physical therapy sessions.

Women's basketball flourished under Coach Andy Landers. He shares with Jack Bauerle the distinction of having the longest tenure of all Georgia's coaches at thirty-four years, and he has won a record 773 games. Landers has won seven SEC Championships and has been to the Final Four five times. There have been many All-Americans but none as notable as Teresa Edwards and Katrina McClain. Edwards is regarded by many as the greatest women's basketball player of all time.

Women's tennis has been under the direction of Jeff Wallace for twenty-seven years and has won National Championships in 1994 and 2000, as well as National Indoor Championships in 1994, 1995, and 2002. Wallace has also won eight SEC Championships.

We started an equestrian team at the University in 2001, and it is recognized today as an emerging sport by the NCAA. Georgia's first and only coach, Meghan Boenig, has been highly successful, winning National Championships in 2003, 2008, 2009, and 2010. The array of championships is tempered by the fact that there are only eighteen schools nationally with equestrian teams and only three in the SEC.

The women's golf team joined the march of championships by winning the national title in 2001 under Todd McCorkle. However, Beans Kelley, who coached women's golf, laid the foundation by winning seven SEC Championships.

Lou Harris-Champer, the women's fast pitch softball coach who was hired in 2000, has produced consistent winners with two SEC Championships in 2003 and 2005. Although it has been awhile, Sid Feldman coached two SEC Championship teams in volleyball in 1985 and 1986. Women's track and field has won SEC Championships in 1995 (outdoors) under John Mitchell and 2006 (indoors and outdoors) under Wayne Norton.

Hugh Durham, who coached men's basketball for seventeen years (1979–95), led the Bulldogs in 1990 to its first and only Southeastern Conference Championship. Durham was Georgia's most successful coach, reaching the Final Four in 1983. He produced such superstars as Dominique Wilkins and Vern Fleming, both of whom

coached are too numerous to mention but there are a few whose performances are the greatest of the great. Courtney Kupets won nine individual National Championships and was named the winner of the Honda-Broderick Trophy in 2009, symbolic of the nation's greatest athlete in all sports. How can I ever forget Karin Lichey in 1996 scoring a perfect 10 in all four events—the first and only Bulldog to ever score a perfect 40. One of my favorite gymnasts was Heather Stepp McCormick who was told by doctors that she would never be able to compete again after a near catastrophic elbow injury. She not only competed but became an All-American and three-time individual NCAA champion and won

Coach Hugh Durham

played several years in the NBA. After the 1990 season, Durham went four years without a NCAA bid. After a lot of anxiety, I decided to replace him in 1995 with Tubby Smith, who had great success at Tulsa. Despite being at Georgia only two years, Smith became one of Georgia's most popular coaches. Both of his teams earned NCAA tournament berths. Smith and his family loved the University but an offer came from Kentucky that he couldn't turn down. Otherwise, I believe Smith would have had a long career at Georgia.

Smith was replaced by his top assistant Ron Jirsa, who coached the team for two years. Jirsa was replaced in 1999 by Jim Harrick, one of the best on-court basketball coaches I have ever known. University President Mike Adams, who had known Harrick at Pepperdine College, was influential in his hiring. In a brief four years (1999–2003), Harrick produced some great teams and basketball fever reached an all-time high. Among his players was Jarvis Hayes, a superstar who played several years in the NBA. Tragically it all came to an end when major recruiting violations, primarily by his son, Jim Harrick Jr., an assistant coach, led to Harrick's resignation.

At the turn of the century, despite the roller coaster

ride in men's basketball, Georgia had one of the best overall athletic programs in the country. In 1998 the Bulldogs finished second (behind Stanford) in the Director's Cup as the best overall athletic program in the country. Stanford, with its multitude of sports, has now won the Director's Cup seventeen straight years as of 2010–2011. In 2001 our program finished third in the nation overall, and in my last year as Athletic Director in 2004, we finished fifth. The Director's Cup is sponsored by Learfield Sports and administered by the National Association of Collegiate Directors of Athletics.

At the same time, Texas A&M created the "excellence in athletics cup" based on an evaluation of intercollegiate programs in eight different categories. Georgia finished first in the SEC. Meanwhile, the University of Florida student newspaper in a league study in 2004 concluded that Georgia was at the top of the conference in getting the "biggest bang for the buck." In essence the study concluded that Georgia most effectively used its resources. The results of all the studies were a point of pride for Georgia's athletics.

The successes of the Georgia athletic programs are proudly displayed in a museum in the lobby of the Butts-Mehre Heritage Hall building, which was completed in 1986. This state-of-the-art facility was a result of a $12 million fund-raiser by Bulldog supporters. In addition to administrative and football coaches' offices, the building houses a separate museum for football. The facility has undergone several renovations since its completion. The most recent in 2011 is a $34 million addition that includes new office space, a football training facility, and a partial indoor football field. Concurrent with the Butts-Mehre renovation, Stegeman Coliseum received a $13 million facelift, providing a top-of-the-line facility for men and women's basketball and women's gymnastics. Other modern athletic facility upgrades include the Jack Turner (longtime alumnus, friend, and athletic board member) Women's Softball Stadium in 2011 and the Spec Towns Track in 2010. All of these facility upgrades were funded by the Athletic Association with private funds. Topflight facilities are necessary to compete in the rugged SEC, the best and most competitive athletic conference in the nation.

The championships won by Georgia's teams competing in intercollegiate athletics at the highest level have been remarkable. Knapp was genuinely supportive of all our programs. During the height of competition, women's basketball coach Andy Landers and women's gymnastics coach Suzanne Yoculan, whose salaries had not kept up with their successes and changing times, threatened to sue the program unless their salaries were dramatically increased. While plans were already underway to give them substantial increases, the coaches were not satisfied and a public controversy erupted. In the final analysis, a meeting with Knapp, me, the two coaches, and their attorneys resolved the issue. In all of the athletic crises we had, Knapp was straightforward and handled situations in what he perceived were in the best interest of the University.

Knapp resigned as president in 1997 after ten years of productive and faithful service in order to join the Aspen Institute in Washington. The institute is a national think tank, designed to "foster values-based leadership, encouraging individuals to reflect on the ideals and ideas that define a good society"

Knapp achieved his goal of making the nation's oldest state-chartered public university "one of the nation's best public universities." He was praised for his leadership in helping to heal the Kemp wounds and "building coalitions between alumni, business and corporate leaders, private donors and state politicians." He was highly respected and established an excellent working relationship with the UGA Foundation, which became a serious issue under his successor. The Georgia State Senate praised Knapp in a resolution, noting that he had "emphasized the importance of teaching… encouraged senior faculty to teach core undergraduate courses and…supported the recognition of teaching excellence" by establishing teaching honors such as "the Meigs Teaching Award and the Russell Undergraduate Teaching Award." At a campus lawn farewell entitled "Good Luck Chuck," he left behind proud University of 30,000 students, 8,500 employees and a budget of more than $600 million.

Knapp was the fourth president I had the privilege to serve. Mike Adams, president of Centre College, succeeded Knapp in 1997. Of the five presidents I served, he became the most difficult to work with, and along with Alonzo Church, one of the most controversial presidents in the history of the University of Georgia.

Dominique Wilkins

The Adams Era

Michael F. Adams became the University of Georgia's twenty-first president in June 1997. Born in Montgomery, Alabama, he lived in Albany, Macon, and Atlanta before moving to Chattanooga to finish high school. His father, Herbert, a very nice gentleman, was a sales manager with Kraft Foods, which explains why the family moved so often.

Adams graduated from David Lipscomb University, a Church of Christ–related school in Nashville, Tennessee. In 1970, he left for The Ohio State University, where he attained two graduate degrees in a relatively new discipline at the time: political communications. The lessons learned from this study served him well in his future endeavors.

He taught at Ohio State for two years before taking a job as chief of staff to Tennessee U.S. Senator Howard Baker from 1976 to 1979. Adams had written his doctoral dissertation on one of Baker's senatorial campaigns and earlier had written his master's thesis on Spiro Agnew's gubernatorial election campaign of 1966. He was so caught up in politics early on that he ran as a Republican for a U.S. House seat in 1980 but was defeated. For the next two years he served as a senior

PENLEY

Michael F. Adams

advisor to Tennessee governor Lamar Alexander before taking his first job in higher education as vice president for university affairs and professor of political communications at Pepperdine University in California. There he came to know men's basketball coach Jim Harrick, and this relationship later would become a controversial subject at the University of Georgia.

In 1988 Adams became president of Centre College, a small, elite, private institution in Kentucky with an enrollment that varied from 800 to 1,200 students. The school is forty miles southwest of Lexington and only ten miles from Perry, the site of the largest Civil War battle in Kentucky. Adams was a surprise choice at Centre College, just as he would later be at the University of Georgia, especially considering his relatively modest professional academic background. Adams's body of research consisted of his master's thesis and doctoral dissertation, neither of which were published. His broad background in politics and fund-raising and not being confined to strictly academe may have been one answer as to why he was chosen to be president. An additional answer may be that he had powerful political patrons in the two U.S. senators from Tennessee, Baker and Alexander.

Adams also had energy, ambition, and personal and political skills. He knew the value of both raising funds and providing opportunities for students to study abroad. During his nine years at Centre he gave the college its best era of fund-raising. He also established residential studies-abroad programs in England and France. At Georgia, he continued to emphasize studies-abroad programs, building on the highly successful art program in Cortona, Italy, created by emeritus UGA art professor John D. "Jack" Kehoe. The Cortona program is in its third decade, and Barbara and I have visited there on a couple occasions. Adams opened a permanent UGA program in Oxford, England, and later in St. Louis, Costa Rica. Funding for the latter facility became highly controversial and was one of a series of crises Adams faced.

Studies Abroad

Barbara and I have experienced firsthand the value of studies-abroad programs. We became involved in one of the newest programs offered by the University. As of 2011, there were, in addition to the three permanent UGA facilities, more than ninety studies-abroad programs in thirty-seven countries led by approximately one hundred University faculty members. From 2009 to 2011, we have participated in perhaps the newest and one of the most successful programs, called Global LEAD.

The program, whose motto is "Don't just go, LEAD!" was founded primarily by Kevin Scott and Garrett Graveson, two of the University's most accomplished graduates, who delivered UGA commencement addresses in 2003 and 2007, respectively. The program, which has been very capably administered by UGA graduates Courtney Doran, Robbie Reese, Beth Ann Schroder, and Joanna Harbin, offers study sites both in South Africa and Greece. Ecuador and the Galapagos Islands are scheduled to be additional study-abroad sites in the future. The University is the academic sponsor of the program and monitors all activities. The UGA staff usually consists of a lead faculty director and a few doctoral students. The students each receive six hours credit, three hours in leadership and three hours in service learning.

LEAD is an acronym for Leadership, Education, Adventure, and Diplomacy. The diplomacy, or service, component makes the program unique. As an example, the students spend time in the township of Cape Town, South Africa, helping to build physical structures for grammar schools and interacting with excitable and appreciative schoolchildren who crave and love the attention offered by the Georgia students. As Kevin Scott said, "Students are building their minds as well as their hearts."

Barbara and I have been twice to Cape Town and once to Greece, interacting and lecturing on the subjects of leadership, teamwork, and overcoming adversity. We are looking forward to being with a new group of students in Ecuador and the Galapagos Islands in the summer of 2012. It has been inspiring to get to know some of these remarkable students and see firsthand how they are touched by what they give. Adams should feel especially good about his work in emphasizing these studies-abroad programs to students who are preparing to work in a shrinking world and learning the rewards of service.

Forceful, Dynamic, and Controversial

Adams's success with the studies-abroad programs confirmed in part what "an Adams's acquaintance at Pepperdine" predicted he would be: "forceful, dynamic and at times...controversial." The latter trait came into play many times during his tenure.

It appears that early on at Pepperdine some of these traits may have come into conflict with a then-young Keith McFarland, who today is a two-time technology CEO and founder of McFarland Strategy Partners Inc. As a youngster in his twenties, McFarland worked under Adams. McFarland wrote a May 15, 2007, article for *Business Week* entitled "In Praise of the Anti-Mentor."

The theme of the article is summed up in its subtitle: "It's important to have role models, but most of us owe a bigger debt of gratitude to the people who teach us by bad example." McFarland did not name the individual or school about which he wrote, but a former dean at Pepperdine suggested Adams was the subject. The dean said, "Everybody in Pepperdine knew who it was, including the president." He said that Adams "was furious when he read the article and threatened the writer."

McFarland had written: "The hot shot vice-president who took over where I worked when I was in my twenties was a great anti-mentor. Arrogant, quick-tempered, and controlling, it took him only six months to turn a great department into a loose collection of warring tribal fiefdoms." McFarland then asked and answered the question, "What did my anti-mentor teach me?" The lessons came after his anti-mentor agreed to honor his request to transfer, but under the condition that the anti-mentor be allowed to inform the president.

McFarland said he later found out the anti-mentor had lied to the president as to why he wanted "to transfer to a different department." McFarland said the lesson taught him "that people, even those you view as untrustworthy, are essentially reliable." But wait, McFarland wrote, "hadn't this person betrayed me by lying to the president about my real motivation for leaving the job?... Yes and that's precisely my point. He acted reliably. I knew he was selfish, manipulative and inse-

President's house

cure, so to expect him to act any other way was really poor judgment on my part."

The article and related information was shared with me by Bob Hope, a highly respected public relations guru of Atlanta. I, too, believe there is much to learn from "anti-mentors." I served as an assistant football coach in the Marine Corps under a colonel who was a good marine officer but a poor head football coach, and I learned many lessons of what not to do when I became a head coach.

Adams, after a four-year stay at Pepperdine, became president of Centre College in 1988. The late Rich Whitt, a writer for more than thirty years with the *Louisville Courier-Journal* and the *Atlanta Journal-Constitution,* wrote a book titled *Behind the Hedges,* which centered on Adams's controversy with University of Georgia alumni, faculty, and primarily its foundation. Whitt had won numerous awards as a reporter, including a Pulitzer Prize with the *Courier-Journal,* and did extensive research into Adams's background and the controversy. He said "one knock on Adams has been that he is hot-tempered and imperious...qualities that did not endear him to Centre's faculty any more than they have at Georgia." After nine years at Centre, Whitt wrote, many at Centre were tired of Adams's "bulldozer tactics." Whitt wrote that a "quiet revolt was being plotted by eighteen senior professors."

After Adams unilaterally made changes to the faculty handbook "in violation of the college's own policy," Whitt wrote, "Adams blamed a dean for making the changes without his permission." Faculty members said "they knew better." Whitt quoted a senior faculty member: "The changes were made at Adams' instruction.... He stood right there and lied to sixteen faculty members who were at the meeting." Whitt said three other faculty members confirmed the professor's recollection of the occasion.

Whitt quoted Charles Vahlkamp, a retired Centre faculty member, who attended the meeting with Adams and recalled "there was a big sigh of relief" when Adams took the UGA job. Vahlkamp further said, "He's good at some aspects, but he is a divisive character. Not a consensus builder." I don't know Vahlkamp or what happened at Centre College, but based on my experience, I do not disagree with his evaluation. I will add that Adams is highly aggressive and ambitious, speaks

very well, has a great ability to say the right things, and knows the power base and how to manipulate it. He used all of those skills in moving from a small private college to a flagship research university.

Adams's style and skills were meshed with good timing in the job search at Georgia. Usually a person who succeeds someone else in an important leadership position is appointed primarily because his or her skill sets are different. Where a previous leader was weak in one area, the selection consensus wants the next person to be strong in the previous deficient skills. Knapp was a great consensus-building president, a learned academician who was well respected by the faculty and all of those who knew him. He was admired for his reserved modesty. The committee may have been looking for a more aggressive, CEO-style administrator who would get things done faster rather than wait to build consensus. Adams was the opposite of Knapp in many ways. He was hands-on, controlling, and (some say) egotistical. Whitt, who also called Adams a "braggart," reported that "journalist Richard Wilson, who had written the 1988 Adams review in the *Louisville Courier-Journal,* recalled getting a telephone call from Adams...to have lunch and chat." Wilson said, "I sat and listened to him for an hour and a half, and all he talked about was the rich and influential people he had met."

Nevertheless Adams possessed qualities that were obviously important to the Regents. Based on his tenure at Centre College, he possessed a strong corporate CEO management style and a strong reputation for fund raising. He had the political support of some key office holders like Governor Zell Miller, who perhaps was influenced by Adams supporters from Tennessee. In turn, Don Leebern, who chaired the search committee for the Board of Regents, was in school at Georgia with Miller and apparently helped sway him in favor of Adams. Leebern was sold on Adams's CEO qualities, and along with Chancellor Stephen Porch, he thought Adams was "a perfect fit" for the job. This support in turn must have had a strong influence on Dan Parker, who headed the search firm for the Board of Regents.

All told, there were sixteen members on the search committee headed by University business professor Betty Whitten. Author Whitt provides a detailed report of how the intriguing selection process unfolded in a chapter on "a presidential search."

Phi Kappa Hall

Regardless, Adams became Georgia's president and despite some bad decisions along the way, he moved forward, improving the University in many areas.

Since Rich Whitt's book *Behind the Hedges* is cited often in dealings with Adams, I have been asked if I know what prompted Whitt to write the book. I don't know for sure, but he had told me that for several months he had accumulated material during the Adams's controversy and wanted to write a series of articles as an investigative journalist for the *Journal-Constitution*. He said he was prevented from pursuing the idea, however. Whitt told me that he saved the mate-

rial, and after he retired from the newspaper, he would use the research as a base for writing a book. Like so many investigative reporters, he had a passion for telling what he believed to be the truth. I was told later by my book publisher, Dick Parker, who met Whitt and discussed the project with him, that he, too, believes that Whitt's passion drove him to investigate the story and write the book.

While the book is basically critical of Adams, it was endorsed by some highly respected academicians, foremost among them being historian Sheldon Hackney, the former provost at Princeton University and former

Meigs Hall

president of the University of Pennsylvania and Tulane University. Hackney was also the former chairman of the National Endowment for the Humanities. His comments on the back cover read: "This authoritative tale of colorful characters thrashing about in a tangled web of compromised moral principles should be required reading for everyone in higher education. *Behind the Hedges* is a clear demonstration that within our universities, the highest ethical precepts should be the foundation of both good politics and effective leadership."

University Master Plan and Campus Expansion

Adams followed Knapp's lead in the development of a new master plan for the campus. The firm of Ayers Saint/Gross of Baltimore was hired during Knapp's last year in 1997. The University campus architects, under Danny Sniff, and the Ayers firm implemented plans to restore historic buildings, address academic space priorities, and most notably, to create more green space.

Among the historic restoration projects was Meigs Hall, which would accommodate the Institute of Higher Education. Old College, the University's oldest permanent building, was renovated and provided office space for the dean and administrators of the Franklin College of Arts and Sciences. Both the old debating societies buildings—Phi Kappa Hall and Demosthenian Hall— also underwent renovation.

Adams "raised some eyebrows," according to Rich Whitt, when he took Knapp's plan of a $2.1-million-renovation of the old Georgia Museum of Art on the main campus to provide offices for campus planning and legal affairs and changed it to a $2.5-million-dollar renovation for offices of the president and his se-

The old library, built in 1862, also held classrooms and a museum. It was later combined with Ivy Hall and would become the Academic Building.

nior staff. The concern of some faculty members and students was it this transformation took place during a time of belt-tightening at the University. As it turned out, it was a good investment, providing upscale offices for the president of a university on the move.

The move from the modest Lustrat House, occupied by the three previous presidents, to the upscale renovation of the new spacious facility fit the pattern of Adams's management style. "The free-spending reputation" Adams was acquiring, Whitt wrote, came on the heels of the $90,000 spent on his inauguration. The Lustrat House, incidentally, became headquarters of the University's legal affairs office. Meanwhile, the Athletic Association spent $220,000 on the president's skybox at the stadium, which also turned out to be a good investment.

Georgia was a quarter-century behind some of the top public institutions around the country in realizing the value of green space, and the University rapidly moved forward with green-space plans. Historic North

Memorial Hall, with a bronze plaque with the names of the university alumni who lost their lives in World War I, opened in 1925 and was approved for a $2.5 million renovation in 2011.

Campus had a complete facelift by changing the parking lot that had occupied old Herty Field into a beautiful park with paths and flower beds, all accentuated by a large aesthetic water fountain. At the base of this green space sits historic Moore College, which underwent restoration to house the Honors Program and the "Foundation Fellows."

Built in 1874, Moore College has a unique and interesting history. It was financed during post–Civil War hard times by the city of Athens in the amount of $25,000 for a new classroom building for the new federal land-grant college. This unique arrangement came about through the efforts of a local physician and University trustee, Dr. Richard Moore. Historian F. N. Boney observed that Moore College is the only "French Second Empire building on campus."

The most impressive structure built during the Adams administration was the $43.6-million student learning center completed in 2003. The facility on Lumpkin Street in central campus is named for Governor Zell

Miller and represents the largest capital project ever undertaken by the University system. In 2007 the Tate Student Center was restored and expanded, including a parking deck that accommodates some 500 cars.

On South Campus, the Paul D. Coverdell Center for Biomedical and Health Sciences, in honor of the late Georgia senator, opened in 2006. Financed partially with federal funds, former President George H. W. Bush and First Lady Barbara Bush visited the campus for the dedication.

In January 2011, the Museum of Art opened its long-anticipated Phase II addition under the superb directorship of William U. Eiland. The new addition adds extensive exhibition and storage space as well as an outdoor sculpture garden to the state's art museum. During a summer reception at the new facility, I joined a group following Eiland, who conducted a splendid tour (he always does) of his pride and joy. Along the way he emphasized the dual designation of the museum. Eiland said that while it's "the official state art museum of Georgia," it is also an "academic museum" with educational ties to the University through the Lamar Dodd School of Art and Design, which moved from North Campus to the East Campus art quad in 2009.

Another green-space project was the conversion of D. W. Brooks Drive to an area of paths, gardens, and lawns. The space that runs from Ag Hill to the plant sciences building is a pleasant, aesthetic north-south walkway, adding to the ambience of the campus.

Campus Arboretum

I was proud to contribute in a small way to the general awareness of campus beauty by chairing a University committee in 2000 that converted the entire campus into an arboretum. It was a little strange for me, a focused former head football coach and athletic director, to chair a University committee consisting of a diverse group of experts in horticulture, forestry, botany, and landscape architecture. I have often said that one of the great benefits of living around a university is, if one has a curiosity about anything, it can be satisfied because there is an expert on everything. There is a joy to learning, and I have often enjoyed auditing courses in history (the Civil War particularly), art history, and theology.

Several years ago my curiosity was aroused about trees and plants, and with no knowledge whatsoever in horticulture, I audited courses under perhaps two of the best professors in one discipline at the University and arguably the nation: Drs. Allan Armitage and Michael Dirr. Both have published more than a dozen books so far and are regarded as the gurus of herbaceous and woody plants, respectively. While serving on the Athens Urban Tree Advisory Committee, I volunteered to chair a committee on "UGA as an Arboretum."

Dirr, a winner of the Meigs Award for teaching and my primary horticulture mentor, had often expressed the opinion that the UGA campus should be designated as an arboretum. I know from experience that, to do anything at the University, there is a process that takes time. It always starts with a committee, and while I had little knowledge at the time about a campus arboretum, I knew something about putting a good group of people together as a team and organizing them to be productive.

I recruited an arboretum committee class comparable to the great recruiting class of 1980 that won the National Championship while producing two consensus All-Americans in Herschel Walker and Terry Hoage. Dirr was my "Walker workhorse." The committee also included Armitage, along with Kim Coder, forestry professor and internationally recognized expert on trees; Dexter Adams, head of the University grounds department; Ingrid Sather, of the USDA Forestry Service; and Danny Sniff, director of campus planning. There were several other outstanding committee members representing various campus disciplines. I basically called the meeting to order and "gave them the ball and let them run with it." Despite the individual talent on the committee, the group worked well together in defining the mission of the arboretum, outlining the goals, and steering the project through the necessary University processes, which took about eighteen months. The project brought a further awareness to the beauty of the campus.

I acquired a special appreciation for the beauty of the University campus after receiving a copy of a letter sent from noted Auburn horticulture professor Dr. Ken Tilt to President Michael Adams in 2001. Tilt wanted Adams to understand the "arboretum treasure" that he, the faculty, and the students had inherited. Tilt called it "an academic and cultural jewel as important as your new museum and performing arts theater." Tilt further

Herty Field, fountain, and Moore College

said that he had attended many campus planning committee sessions and "when the question was asked of the members what they would like for their city and campus to look like...they always responded UNC Chapel Hill and UGA Athens." The compliment stirred my campus pride.

The Georgia campus arboretum is a point of pride for all the committee members, especially the energetic Dirr, who labeled the trees on campus and wrote the brochure for the campus arboretum walking tour. The brochure contains maps of the three campus walks: the North Campus (0.5 miles), the Central Campus (1.2 miles), and the South Campus (2.5 miles). There are a total of 154 labeled trees on the entire campus walk. The campus arboretum is indeed a University treasure.

Reorganizing Academe

Aside from the beauty of the campus, Adams had formed some reorganizing plans for the academic aspects of the University. In January 1999 he announced plans to add four schools and colleges to the Athens campus. He was successful in adding three of the four.

He backed away from his proposal to dismantle the Grady College of Journalism and replace it with a new College of Journalism that would include "rhetorical studies, speech, and technology." There was a virtual revolt by the faculty and prominent alumni from across the state and the nation who had received their training at the Grady School. The faculty was outraged that Adams had not bothered to consult with them or even Dean Tom Russell. Rich Whitt wrote in *Behind the Hedges* that the dean was informed of the plan as late as the night before the announcement. The strained relationship between Russell and Adams eventually led to the resignation of the highly regarded dean.

Nevertheless, in 2001, Adams's initiative led to the establishment of the School of Public and International Affairs and the College of Environment and Design. In 2005 the College of Public Health was established, and in 2007 the Institute of Ecology was changed to the Eugene P. Odum School of Ecology in honor and memory of the "father of modern ecology."

Perhaps even more significant, Adams was able to form a partnership with the Medical College of Georgia to enroll medical students at the University. The first class enrolled in 2010–2011, attending classes in the "partnership building down by the river." Starting in 2011–2012, classes were held at the newly renovated Navy Supply Corps School that had been deeded back to the University when the navy closed shop in Athens. It is now called the UGA Health Sciences Campus.

Equally important, Adams persuaded the Board of Regents to expand the longtime existing UGA engineering school that had focused on agriculture and the environment and add the disciplines of civil, mechanical, and electrical engineering. The additional engineering courses are to be implemented by 2014. As expected, the issue was highly controversial, with strong objections raised by the faculty and alumni of Georgia Tech and Southern Polytechnic State University. To Adams's credit, he brought the new engineering disciplines to the University just as he had done the medical school.

In 2011 Adams also negotiated the reunion of two University foundations—the traditional UGA Foundation and the newly formed Arch Foundation. The cause of the split was the result of a storm that took place within the UGA Foundation over Adams's "spending, compensation, and accountability," according to Rich Whitt. The controversy resulted in the Board of Regents' disassociating the UGA Foundation from the University as its fund-raising arm, ending a seventy-year relationship. Adams formed the Arch Foundation in its place.

Having two foundations for seven years supporting the University was reflective of the divisions that existed over Adams, so the merging of the two was best for the University and an absolute necessity for the proposed $1 billion fund-raiser to follow.

The UGA Foundation and President Adams

The initial friction between the UGA Foundation and Adams was over the president's spending habits. As Rich Whitt points out in *Behind the Hedges,* the Foundation had "few rules about the president's spending of privately raised money in an account over which he had direct control." The assumption was that Adams would use the discretionary fund in "the best interest of the University" as his predecessor, Chuck Knapp, "a frugal caretaker," had done. Adams, however, "brought a different attitude." Whitt disclosed that Adams used the president's discretionary fund for "air fare that appeared personal, dinners at expensive restaurants for himself and his staff...even a graduation party for his son's law school class." Many members of the Foundation were "outraged," Whitt wrote, and they began to tighten the rules on how money was spent. This in turn seemed to irritate Adams.

The late Griffin Bell, an Atlanta attorney and former U.S. Attorney General, was the counsel for the Foundation. He said that the trustees had a "fiduciary duty...to the Foundation donors to ensure their gifts are properly used." Tension that built up over a period of time between the Foundation and Adams was exacerbated by the "shabby way," as many put it, that Adams dealt with me.

Some of my personal experiences with Adams are documented in my book, *Dooley: My 40 Years at Georgia.* I have also expressed myself concerning Adams in Whitt's book, *Behind the Hedges.* There are other incidents not revealed in either book that may have a future place of expression but are not appropriate at this writing.

Broad Street, Athens

It is well documented that Adams refused to honor my request for a contract extension, and the manner in which he did so caused an uproar among many Georgia supporters, including many members of the Board of Trustees.

The controversy escalated when billboards appeared and petitions circulated condemning Adams. Some 500 people asked that their names be withdrawn from the $500-million fund-raising campaign that was just getting under way. Herschel Walker had earlier agreed to be on the campaign committee, but he resigned. ESPN showed up to do an *Outside the Lines* documentary about the controversy. Adams seized the moment and, using his political communication background, painted the controversy as "academics versus athletics." Stating "this is about who will control the University…the athletic side of the house or the University side of the house." It was a clever spin, and as Griffin Bell stated, "The newspaper bought into it." The *Atlanta Journal-Constitution* became a staunch defender of Adams.

Seeing that the Adams spin was having a positive effect for him but a negative effect on the University, I made a public statement that the "academics versus athletics" position is a false portrayal of the controversy and that "academics is always at the forefront of the University." I then asked everyone who might have issues with Adams not to use my name in connection with any disagreements. Some described this statement as my "calling off the Dawgs." Adams took the opportunity to thank me publicly and to seek my advice on how to bring the Bulldog Nation and University together. We met, and at the meeting, I suggested that a one-year extension of my job as athletic director might be a good-faith effort that would sit well with the Georgia people. Adams said he would think about it, but he dismissed the idea. I have said often that he seeks my advice publicly but does not take it privately.

During our meeting, Adams mentioned an ongoing financial audit by the Foundation. He asked me about it, and I told him I was not privy to the audit or the Foundation's reasons for it. He suggested I get the Foundation to call off the audit. There was no doubt Adams was proposing to strike a deal. I again reemphasized that the action of the Foundation was beyond my control.

Foundation Audit

About a month after Adams's initial decision not to renew my contract, I heard that the Foundation leaders had asked their legal counsel, the King & Spalding law firm, to hire an outside auditor who would "prove or disprove the serious concerns of a growing number of the Foundation trustees." King & Spalding hired the fraud and forensics investigations unit of Deloitte & Touche to investigate. I knew nothing about the investigation at the time, and when I inquired about the rumors, I was told by two Foundation members, Billy Payne and Wyck Knox, that it was none of my business. I respected both of them and dropped the matter, until Adams mentioned it in our private conversation mentioned above.

When the audit was released to the public, the revelation that received the most attention was a $250,000 "secret deal" with former coach Jim Donnan. Coach Donnan had become a hot commodity after the 1997 season, when the team finished 10–2 and had beat Florida for the first time in eight years. We negotiated a new contract for Donnan, giving him almost everything he asked for. However, the negotiation bogged down when I was not in favor of one of his contract demands. I did not know it at the time, but the stalemate was broken when Adams, through alumnus Jim Nalley, agreed to a secret deal with Donnan and his agent Richard Howell. The agreement—which was kept from me, our law firm, and the athletic board (which traditionally authorizes such expenditures)—called for Donnan to be paid about a quarter million dollars should he be fired with three or more years left on his contract, a condition not likely to happen. Ironically, however, that is exactly what happened. When the secret deal came to my attention, I was shocked. It was also shocking to most of the athletic board members as well as to our law firm, which had negotiated the standard contract.

Adams's public response to the secret deal was that "in hindsight I probably would have handled it differently." So when the audit was released to the public, I was well aware of the secret deal. The rest of the audit finding was very surprising to me. Whitt included the complete fifty-eight-page audit as an appendix in *Behind the Hedges,* which in summary concluded the following:

Adams Expenses: Adams spent $10,000 of the Foundation's money to host a commencement luncheon at the president's house for the 2002 law school graduation class that included his son David. The luncheon was by "invitation only" and had never been done by Adams before or since. With no recourse to the finding, Adams paid the money back.

The audit also found that Adams "knowingly provided inaccurate and/or incomplete documentation to the Foundation" when he handed out free tickets to football games to friends and listed the friends as major gift prospects. Earlier some Foundation members had met with Adams to question some expenses and propose more accountability. Adams did not like the idea but said that, "realizing the level of concern," he accepted them.

It appears there is a correlation between Adams's discretionary funds being scrutinized by the Foundation and his request for a substantial raise in his expense money from the Athletic Association. As part of the president's discretionary fund, the Athletic Association had traditionally set aside in its annual budget funds for the president to travel, entertain, and take part in athletic-related events. In 2001, $25,000 was set aside for Adams, a round number that had been fairly constant for several years, with periodic inflation adjustments. Adams's predecessor, Chuck Knapp, had operated with that amount in his athletic expense account for ten years.

In 2003 that amount tripled to $75,000. In essence, the $50,000 increase requested by the president's office over a two-year period became a part of his discretionary fund. It would appear the additional funding enabled him to ease the financial scrutiny by the Foundation.

As of 2011, the $75,000 in the Athletic Association budget for Adams's "discretionary fund" had grown to $125,000 a year—a substantial money source for the president, with no scrutiny. The amount does not include money from bowl revenue that is used by the president to "entertain." Whitt wrote that at the 2008 Sugar Bowl he spent "$138,000 on himself and a few dozen friends to whoop it up in New Orleans." Adams defended the expenditure by saying it's "Athletic Association money...all part of the bowl culture."

The auditors also found that Adams had "misled Foundation trustees" to win himself a substantial pay increase in 2002 and suggested "there was a deliberate act to conceal Adams's pay increase from the faculty and staff."

The auditors suggested Adams turned a blind eye to a mistake in his deferred compensation package that caused him to be overpaid. On another occasion Adams received a $12,000 temporary annuity as a bridge to a new retirement plan and never stopped receiving the money when the retirement funding kicked in. "When confronted, Adams reimbursed the state by a payroll deduction in December 2004, as he had done previously with the Foundation."

The report also indicated that Adams "wasn't always upfront" in his efforts to get the Foundation to supplement his pay. Case in point, Adams said he had been offered the Ohio State job with a salary of "$850,000 to $1 million a year and that he helped steer the job to UGA provost Karen Holbrook after he turned it down." Both assertions were "flatly refuted" by James Patterson, chair of the Ohio State search committee, according to Rich Whitt.

Mary Adams's Compensation: The report addressed the $48,000-per-year income that was paid to Mary Adams by the Foundation. Rich Whitt stated that Adams felt his wife should be reimbursed "for her efforts on behalf of the University of Georgia" and suggested to then-Foundation chairman Jim Nalley that she be put on the Foundation payroll. "Nalley thought it was a bad idea, as did other members of the Foundation Executive Committee."

In 2000, the new chairman, Pat Pittard, was in favor of the idea after it was brought up by Adams. Whitt stated that Don Leebern funded the compensation with a tax write-off donation to the Foundation. Part of the $48,000 compensation included an $800 monthly expense allowance that Pittard later agreed (after Adams's request) to put the expense allowance in Mary Adams's supplemental retirement account. The auditors concluded that Pittard violated Foundation procedures by "agreeing to put the $800 per month expense allowance into a retirement account without getting Executive Committee approval."

Hank Huckaby: The auditors concluded the Foundation Executive Committee erred in approving a $30,000 honorarium to the University's senior vice president Henry M. "Hank" Huckaby for working six months for

Park Hall

Governor-Elect Sonny Perdue as part of his transition team. Huckaby is described as "one of Adam's staunchest defenders" by Rich Whitt.

Adams appointed Huckaby as senior vice president of finance and administration for UGA from 2000 to 2006. Governor Perdue in turn was a loyal and staunch defender of Adams since the president publicly supported Perdue for governor when he was a dark-horse candidate. Adams brought Perdue to a Georgia basketball game at which the incumbent governor, Roy Barnes, was in attendance. It was a shocking gesture

to many but turned out to be perhaps the best political decision Adams ever made.

The Alumni Center: The auditors blamed Adams for micromanaging the alumni center project that "cost the University $1.4 million in architectural fees with nearly nothing to show for it." According to Whitt, plans had already been in progress "for a three-building, $8.6-million-dollar project that six years later became a $74 million project that has never been built." Whitt called the episode "a tale of intrigue, mismanagement, and finger pointing." The journey included using five different architects, the last one a friend of Adams, Al Filoni of Pittsburgh, who was paid $75,000 by the Foundation (after the University refused to pay) to serve "as a consultant," according to UGA officials. The responsibility for the project shifted from the University under campus planner Danny Sniff to the UGA Real Estate Foundation (a subsidiary of the UGA Foundation) under JoAnn Chitty. The audit "pointed the finger at Adams as the one person who had the final say on every design...and single-handedly put Mr. Filoni to work on the design and terminated the Carusi Firm." The report concluded that Adams "violated purchasing procedures when he hired Filoni without going through proper purchasing procedures.... Bringing in an old friend...creates an appearance of impropriety on the part of Dr. Adams."

The Ecolodge: The purchase of a studies-abroad facility in Saint Louis, Costa Rica, in 2002 is another intriguing story involving Adams. This time it primarily included Vice President of Development Kathryn Costello and Senior Vice President of External Affairs Steve Wrigley. To his credit, Adams was a strong believer in studies-abroad programs both at Centre College and the University. Permanent facilities had long been established in Cortona, Italy, and Adams added a facility in Oxford, England. He wanted to add another facility in Costa Rica, called the Ecolodge, after finding out the 170-acre facility long used by faculty and students was for sale. Costello received the approval of the Foundation Executive Committee to agree on a $40,000 earnest money payment of the $895,000 purchase price.

After it was determined by the Real Estate Foundation that purchasing the facility would cause negative cash flow, the plan was put on hold. At this point Adams stepped in and "challenged Costello and others that if they could raise $500,000 he would (without authorization, according to auditors) commit $500,000 of Foundation funds." Later, Costello, confident the $500,000 challenge had been met, authorized the purchase without Foundation approval, which in turn was grounds for her dismissal. The auditors blamed Costello for making the purchase but concluded that Adams, in addition to being at fault in committing the matching money of the Foundation, "also failed to properly manage" Costello.

The scenario becomes more intriguing when Wrigley called fund-raising consultant Charles Witzleben (who had worked at Centre College with Adams)

about employment for Costello. According to Witzleben, Rich Whitt wrote, the phone conversation started with Wrigley's saying, "Charlie this is Steve. I have a question to ask and I think I know the answer, but I have been asked to make the call. Would you employ Kathy Costello as a consultant to your company?" Witzleben replied, "No!" In the University response to the auditor's report on the subject, both Adams and Wrigley "confessed to a poor recall to any topic dating back to 2001 and 2002 when the Ecolodge transaction occurred."

Witzleben later told Whitt about the Wrigley conversation, reiterating that "quite frankly Steve (Wrigley) was asked to call me," referring to the opening conversation by Wrigley when he said, "I've been asked to call."

The audit report was completed in October 2003 and "concluded Adams had mishandled Foundation money." It also found fault with "the lax oversight of spending by the Foundation trustees." The "weak oversight" conclusion left the Foundation vulnerable to criticism from both the media and the Regents, and both made good use of the opportunity to point their fingers at the Foundation.

Nevertheless, the report "accused Adams of using Foundation assets to benefit himself, his friends, and his family members." The report also called into question his honesty in dealing with the Foundation, suggesting "he lied about the job offer from The Ohio State University in order to get a salary increase from the Foundation."

An Audit Backfire

In the final analysis, the report did not injure Adams, which was a far different result from what many Foundation trustees had anticipated. Some members thought it would trigger a criminal investigation while others were confident it would lead to Adams's dismissal.

The Regents interpreted the report as "interfering in their external affairs" and criticized the Foundation, saying its own internal procedures and practices contributed to some of the "concerns and confusions." Some Regents publicly called the report "unprofessional and biased...an allegation that went unanswered by the auditors at the time."

In his response to the audit, Adams admitted that

he had made some mistakes, like "the planning of the newest alumni development center," and the "appearance of impropriety" in expensing the $10,000 party for his son's law school class. However, for the most part, he was, according to Whitt, "dismissive of the report."

In addition to Adams's response to the audit, his management team responded with a much firmer stance, concluding that the Deloitte & Touche report contained factual errors and "is not the result of a straight-forward process.... In addition to outright errors the report contains numerous instances of subjective judgment that Mr. Fancher is in no position to make." The assertion that Adams focused on his compensation to the exclusion of other issues is "a totally inaccurate depiction of Dr. Adams." The management report concluded by submitting "the Board of Regents should not accept the D&T reports as credible on the issues it attempts to address." The Regents found Adams and the senior management report to be "far more credible" than the D&T report and pledged their "total and complete support for President Adams."

There were many critics of the Regents for ignoring the findings of the D&T auditors, but none were more outspoken then former University of Virginia head football coach and UGA Senior Associate Athletic Director Dick Bestwick, who periodically writes a column on the editorial page of the *Athens Banner-Herald.* Bestwick, in a letter to the Regents, wrote, "It is incomprehensible to me that you would take issue with the objectivity of a Deloitte & Touche audit but give credence to what Mike Adams and his five sycophants have to say as being objective." He added, "Anything said or claimed to have been done by Mike Adams had to be viewed with a great deal of skepticism. Honesty and integrity are two virtues sadly lacking in Mike Adams's character."

Meanwhile, Deloitte & Touche did not respond to the criticism hurled at the report by Adams, his senior management team, and the Board of Regents, but the firm did respond later to investigative reporter Rich Whitt. J. Donald Fancher, Deloitte & Touche regional managing partner of forensic services, explained why the auditors remained quiet. "The report was intended to be objective," he told Whitt. "It was received that way in my mind because of the politics surrounding the situation. But nonetheless, our effort was to be very objective and to present as much of the information as

we could, but obviously the president and his lieutenants came back with a very derogatory and one-sided response to everything. I think there were lies, quite frankly... [and] many other issues they skirted and never really addressed."

I was not privy at the time to the details of the auditors' findings or to the response by the UGA staff, but as athletic director, I was personally involved on one occasion in the report, and based on my experience with that one incident, the University's legal counsel Steve Shewmaker later misrepresented what took place.

Shewmaker was representing Adams in a meeting held in a conference room next to my office as to how best to address Adams's "under the table deal" with Coach Donnan that was going to cost the Association over $250,000. In addition to Shewmaker and me, three other lawyers were at the meeting: Ed Tolley, representing the Athletic Association; Floyd Newton, representing the Foundation; and Nick Chilivis, my friend and personal attorney. Shewmaker shocked all of us by suggesting that, to avoid public exposure of the issue, the money should be absorbed in the Athletic Association budget and not brought before the Board. I remember thinking at the time that this sounded like a Watergate-type cover-up. The attorneys immediately called Shewmaker's hand on the idea and required that it be brought before the Athletic Board. The Athletic Board ended up authorizing the payment to Donnan.

Shewmaker responded to the audit—which essentially accused him of suggesting a cover-up of the payment—by denying the accusation. To confirm my memory of the meeting, I contacted the other three attorneys individually. They were all in agreement that Shewmaker essentially proposed to cover up the payment to the public by suggesting I absorb the money in the Athletic Association. I had earlier suggested that Shewmaker must have a "short memory," but upon reflection I am not so sure.

Regents Retaliation

Behind the Hedges author Rich Whitt concluded that the Regents were so irritated with the Foundation that they required "all schools in the system to come up with new operating agreements in an effort to restrict the Foun-

The magnificent $42 million Richard B. Russell Special Collections Library will be dedicated in February 2012 and will include the Hargrett Rare Book and Manuscript Library, the Walter J. Brown Archives, and the Peabody Awards Collection.

dation's authority." This affront eventually led to the Regents' disassociating from the Foundation and calling upon Adams to form a new official support unit, which became known as the Arch Foundation.

When the Regents' decision was announced, Regents Vice Chairman Joel O. Wooten accused the Foundation of "thumbing its nose at the Regents," according to Whitt, by not signing a memorandum of understanding between UGA and the Foundation. Wooten said, in essence, according to Whitt, that all institutions in the system had signed such memoranda except the University of Georgia. Whitt called the rationale "a sham," proving that at "least half a dozen schools, including Georgia Tech and the Medical College had not inked the agreements when Wooten made the statement."

The decision to disassociate from the Foundation and the negative response by the Regents to the audit led to the biggest split among friends and supporters I have seen in my forty-plus years of serving the institution. Respected individuals on both sides had harsh

words to say about the situation. Highly respected University of Georgia graduate Jim Blanchard (BBA 1963; LLB 1965), who had served as chairman and CEO of Synovous, informed Adams he would no longer serve on the "Archway to Excellence (fund-raising) campaign." Blanchard, a Foundation leader, uncharacteristically issued this statement upon the Regents' decision to disassociate from the Foundation: "Consider me an adversary rather than an ally. The system of government of our University system is broken and I intend to be part of the effort to fix it." Furthermore, he called the Regents' action "an abomination and the act of a bully." Joel Wooten of Columbus, vice chair of the Foundation and a friend of Blanchard, responded by saying, according to Whitt, it was "the Foundation trustees who were being bullies…a certain group of the trustees never stopped their efforts to frustrate the administration of the University of Georgia." Former U.S. Attorney General Griffin Bell, representing the Foundation, said he knew "there was a great celebration of the Regents when they expelled the Foundation...and no reason to do it. All they had to do was make peace.... We just got the backhand is what we got."

While time has healed some wounds, the scars from the controversy will remain forever. The UGA Foundation and the Arch Foundation, after seven years of separation, came back together in May 2011. This is a great milestone for the University, but the seven-year split points out the division among friends. It appears Adams was willing to agree to the unification in order to include the much-needed old Foundation in a new fund-raising campaign.

The UGA Foundation had continued to manage an endowment of approximately $540 million despite the fact it was not deemed an official fund-raising arm by the University. It annually provided substantial funding to much-needed UGA projects. Actually the old UGA Foundation was receiving more funds annually than the Arch Foundation, the official fund-raising arm of the University. By combining the two foundations, the total endowment is around $620 million at the end of 2011.

Coaches Donnan, Richt, and Harrick

Meanwhile, there was plenty of public attention given to the coaching controversy surrounding Georgia's two most visible and financially prosperous sports: football and men's basketball.

After Jim Donnan went 10–2 and beat Florida in 1997, his next three years never reached the high standard of that year. Of special concern was losing to Georgia Tech three years in a row: 1998, 1999, and 2000. Donnan, whose public relations skills never matched his coaching skills, fell out of grace with Adams, so I knew the long-term future for Donnan at Georgia was not good. Consequently, out of respect for Donnan, I recommended to President Adams that Donnan be given one more year, hoping that would give Donnan time to leave gracefully with a job offer. Adams did not approve my recommendation, which was his prerogative. Donnan was disappointed with the rejection and became irritated when, at a press conference, Adams partly justified his decision by hinting there were drug and other discipline problems that Donnan was not ad-

dressing on the team. Later, Adams and I were in sync with the hiring of a replacement for Jim Donnan.

Later Adams and I were in sync with the hiring of a replacement for Jim Donnan. I hired Chuck Neinas as a consultant, and he suggested a few top candidates that included Mark Richt, offensive coordinator at Florida State, who, at the time, was perhaps the best prospective head coach in the country among assistant coaches. After I had visited with Coach Richt in New York in early December, I arranged to fly to Tallahassee with President Adams for a follow-up interview. We both agreed that Richt was the best choice, and I hired him. However, it was during the trip down and back and during the interview that a problem arose with me and my contract discussion with Adams that eventually led to the controversy over my future at UGA. While we had no disagreement about the hiring of Richt, that was not the case with the hiring of basketball coach Jim Harrick.

The Hiring of Jim Harrick

In 1999, after the dismissal of our basketball coach, Ron Jirsa, I put together a small in-house committee to start the search for a new basketball coach. After extensive research we boiled the list down to three coaches, with Mike Brey of Delaware the leading candidate. Adams called me and said he wanted Jim Harrick on the short list. Harrick had an excellent record as a coach and had won a National Championship at UCLA. I explained to Adams that we did not have him on the list because of his past transgressions. He had been fired at UCLA for falsifying expense accounts and allegedly lying during the investigation. Since Adams had known him at Pepperdine, he politely insisted we have him on the short list.

My choice was Mike Brey, who had worked several years under Mike Krzyzewski at Duke and had an excellent reputation in the athletic world as a fine coach with solid character. In the interview it was obvious to Brey that Adams was less than excited about him, causing Brey to withdraw his name from consideration.

This left the door open for Harrick. He and his wife, Sally, were impressive in the interview, admitting convincingly he had made mistakes and had learned his lesson at UCLA. He was hired, and after four years

Coach Mark Richt

at UGA and much promise on the court, it all came to a tragic end. Harrick hired his son, Jim Harrick Jr., to be an assistant coach. The younger Harrick was found to have violated NCAA rules, and he made a mockery of a regularly scheduled course in basketball with a twenty-question final exam asking such questions as, "How many points does a 3-point field goal account for in a basketball game?"

Eventually Harrick Sr. resigned, which solved a lot of the problems but not all of them. We still had to deal with the NCAA, and a hearing was set in Indianapolis to address the charges. Because we had pulled the basketball team out of the SEC and NCAA tournaments and performed other self-imposed penalties, the NCAA did not take away any scholarships, but the University was placed on probation for four years and wins in the 2002 and 2003 seasons were forfeited in which six ineligible players had participated.

Harrick was replaced with Dennis Felton, who had won two conference championships at Western Kentucky and had an impressive overall record against Kentucky, which was coached at the time by our former head coach, Tubby Smith.

Faculty No Confidence

Meanwhile, the faculty was in a quiet uproar over Adams, and that eventually became a public expression of concern. Respected University biology and botany professor Barry Palevitz told author Rich Whitt that many of the faculty had become "disenchanted with Adams long before the Dooley crisis." They saw him as a CEO-type person, "aloof and unapproachable." Palevitz said, however, that Adams had a hard act to follow in Knapp, whom he described as "a faculty president who cared about academics and the day-to-day running of the University."

Adams installed a campus provost in Dr. Karen Holbrook, formerly of the University of Florida, who turned out to be one of the best hires he ever made at the University. She was well respected by the faculty as well as all who knew her. Adams and Holbrook were a good team. Relations soured, however, when Holbrook went to The Ohio State University as president and later found out about Adams's secret meeting with OSU while she was a candidate for the job.

Palevitz thought my situation was a "catalyst" that sparked some real unrest from the faculty. It was "not that the faculty rose up in support of Dooley," Palevitz told Whitt. "It was over the bad publicity and the embarrassing fight with the Foundation. This was not about athletics versus academics. If the newspapers put it in that context they were woefully wrong." Palevitz added, "The faculty was upset at the portrayal in the media as a war between academics and athletics with the president standing up for academics. That was flat-out wrong. The faculty got angry that it was being portrayed that way." Adams's political communications background spun it that way, and many in the media bought it.

The faculty senate took a poll in February 2004 of the Franklin College of Arts and Sciences faculty (UGA's largest college) about Adams's performance. Approximately 64 percent of the faculty participated, and of those, 70 percent gave Adams a no-confidence vote. Fifteen percent abstained, and only 15 percent expressed confidence in the president. Seventy-four percent responded positively to the question should the faculty senate express a statement about Adams's leadership. The approximately one-thousand-word faculty statement was, according to Rich Whitt, "another searing indictment" of Adams, questioning not only his "extravagant spending but his moral fiber."

The statement contained many comments by the "331 faculty members who gave Adams a no confidence vote." One respondent was concerned about Adams so-called CEO style and stated, "[A] University president of a flagship institution should be more like a leader and exemplar to the faculty." Others spoke to Adams leadership. One respondent stated, "There is an extreme lack of trust and confidence in the leadership of President Adams." Another said, "Leadership is not a word I would associate with Michael Adams."

When the faculty survey was released, it received relatively little notice by the media, and Adams made a statement that he took the survey as "constructive criticism," saying, "As we grow in mutual understanding of our concerns…I trust that confidence in our direction and decision-making processes will grow." Professor Nancy Felson, faculty senate president at the time, was disappointed in Adams's response and told Whitt, "It was treated as a trivial thing…he was self-aggrandizing. Some people felt he was aloof, non-academic. He was treating the place like he was the CEO."

While Felson was "disheartened" at the reaction of the "no confidence vote," the fact of the matter is that historically, according to American Council on Education attorney Sheldon Steinbach, the vote had little impact on Adams. Steinbach told the *Atlanta Journal-Constitution*, "Usually presidents have support of their employers (Board of Regents and the governor) by the time a grievance has reached a vote."

Adams: A Survivor

With such widespread discontent over Adams, many wondered how he was able to survive. I believe the answer lies in his political skill and his early courting of Governor Sonny Perdue in his underdog election bid.

Governor Perdue was loyal to Adams, rejecting every attempt by anyone to convince him that, in the best interest of the University, Adams needed to go. With the governor on board and certain key Regents (like Don Leebern) who championed his hiring, Adams has been able to withstand the pressure.

Adams once told me that he did not believe that Perdue, when he became governor, would look favorably upon the arrangement of Leebern's living with Georgia gymnastics coach Suzanne Yoculan while he was still married to Betsy Leebern, who lived in Columbus. This arrangement was a challenge for everyone, especially me. My wife, Barbara, came down hard on me, saying, "If [Yoculan] had been a male coach at Georgia living with a married women, he would have been fired immediately."

My view has always been that a person's private and personal life is their choosing; however, there is little argument regarding Barbara's point. There is a public responsibility to the University and the Athletic Association on high-profile individuals within department. In retrospect we (President Adams, myself, and the Regents) all should have made a just decision that would uphold the integrity of the University. I regret that I did not take a firm stand on this issue.

But let me say Don Leebern was one of my most valuable supporters when I became Georgia's head coach. Don and his wife, Betsy, were close friends of Barbara and mine for almost forty years. Unfortunately, circumstances change and people change. I understand that and accept it, but I regret that I lost a valued friend in the process.

I did hear from many people complaining about the Leeborn Yoculan arrangement, and their questions prompted me to ask Adams for advice on how he responds to the controversy. He told me, "There are certain things beyond me." He did imply and many felt when Leebern's time on the board was up after a second term that Perdue, admired for his stands on ethics, would not reappoint him. To the shock of many, Perdue did reappoint Leebern, and the governor received tough private criticism from some prominent and respected people. Adams told me that despite the fact that he agreed with many of my concerns, but added, you "can count on him when you need something done that requires Regents' approval."

Staunch Republican Fred Cooper, a former member of the UGA and Arch Foundations and the Board of Regents and regarded as a Perdue confidant, at the time had perhaps the best answer. He told me that Perdue reappointed Leebern because "he would help him control the Board of Regents." Adams's power base was the governor, Leebern, and a few key Regents.

Some believe Adams is off to a good start politically by the way he was able to work with the new governor in the appointment of Henry "Hank" Huckaby as the new university system chancellor. Huckaby was a surprise appointment with a relatively modest academic and leadership background for the position. He does have undergraduate and master's degrees from Georgia State University. His experience in leadership is confined to budget management at the state and the university levels. Often described as a protégé of Zell Miller, Huckaby has extensive political experience: serving as a newly elected state representative and serving previously for six months as part of the transition team (on loan from the University) of Governor Perdue. Huckaby was appointed by Adams as senior vice president of finance at the University, where he served, according to Whitt, as a "loyal and stanch defender of Adams" from 2002 to 2006.

Huckaby's surprise appointment as chancellor was motivated (according to an insider) primarily by Governor Nathan Deal, with support from former Governor Sonny Perdue and his strong political influence on the many Regents the former governor had appointed. This scenario was augmented by Adams, who took a lead role on the selection committee. The fact that two previous chancellors lacked experience in the political process and found themselves unable to get along well with the legislature also added to this shift to a political chancellor. Since the previous chancellor, Erroll B. Davis Jr., did not come out of academia, there have been no complaints over Huckaby's modest professional academic background.

My working experiences with Huckaby dealt with matters pertaining to athletics, and these were always positive. I found him to be competent in his job as vice president for finance and a staunch supporter of and beholder to his boss. Another Adams supporter, Steve Wrigley—a longtime staff member at the University, including vice president for external affairs under Adams—assists Huckaby as the executive vice chancellor. Like Huckaby, Wrigley is a Zell Miller protégé. Overall, both have done good work for the University and should make a good team in the chancellor's office. They will work well with the legislative and political powers.

Generally, people see Huckaby's appointment as very positive, but many question how well he will handle his job as Adams's superior, because he answered to Adams for so long. Some see the appointment as a pathway Adams will use that will eventually lead him to the chancellor's office at the conclusion of Huckaby's tenure, despite what currently would be a substantial salary reduction. Others, with good reasoning, feel Adams already has the best of both worlds: a high-power lucrative job at the University with a virtually unlimited expense account and perks.

Many critics of Adams believe the reason that he has stayed at Georgia so long because he is no longer marketable in the world of academia, considering his track record. He has, of course, a top job at Georgia, and he wouldn't leave unless he were summoned to a unique position that would give him greater exposure, prestige, and financial rewards. One such job would be president of the National Collegiate Athletic Association (NCAA), which was recently filled by former University of Washington and LSU president Dr. Mark A. Emmert.

Adams: NCAA President

Adams was mentioned as a candidate when the NCAA job was open in 2010 after the death of the very competent Myles Brand. Adams publicly denied any interest in the position, but those who attended the January 2010 NCAA convention in Atlanta, where Adams spoke as president of the NCAA Executive Committee, were convinced that he was clearly seeking the position. Former Marshall football coach and longtime athletic director Jack Lengyel (Missouri University and the US Naval Academy) is highly respected in athletic administration circles. He attended the Atlanta convention and heard Adams speak. He told me and many associates that Adams's speech was tailored to seek the NCAA presidency by focusing on what needed to be done to improve the organization.

In the middle of the search for the new NCAA president, Adams resigned as president of the NCAA Executive Committee. The surprise resignation caused many close to the inner workings of the NCAA to ask why Adams, as executive committee president, resigned from a prestigious two-year position with six months remaining in his term. They could only reason that since he was ineligible for the NCAA presidency in his current position, he resigned so that he would be in a position to be "drafted" into the presidency, considering his public stance of not seeking the NCAA position.

The fact that Adams was mentioned as a candidate brought quiet but strong reaction from many. The feelings of many in intercollegiate athletics and academic circles was best summed up in a sports editorial piece by the highly respected *Boston Globe* columnist Bob Ryan on March 28, 2010. Ryan said that normally he would not concern himself with the selection of the NCAA president, but he feared the selection committee would make a "colossal mistake" if they chose Michael Adams. Ryan traced Adams's bout with the UGA Foundation and quoted prominent lawyers Robert Miller and James Ponsoldt on the Deloitte & Touche audit report. Miller said if Adams had been "a senior executive of a major corporation this report would have removed him from office in 24 hours." UGA law school professor James Ponsoldt, who has a background as a prosecutor, said, "There is enough in the audit to convene a grand jury."

Bob Ryan traced Adams's credentials, describing him as not an academic but "a spinmeister...a clever and ruthless politician." He further said, "He is not a leader...he is a schemer and an intimidator."

Ryan also cited the faculty no-confidence vote and recommended Rich Whitt's book *Behind the Hedges* to his readers. Ryan also quoted "an industry insider... and spreader of the anti-Adams gospel that if one tenth of what's in that book is true...the man must be stopped." The scathing article closed the door on whatever chances Adams might have had of being drafted for the NCAA position.

Renee Kaswan

While a public controversy raged in 2003 over the Deloitte & Touche audit and Adams's not renewing my contract, there was a quiet controversy going on over an invention by former veterinary professor Renee Kaswan. Rich Whitt devoted a chapter in his book to the subject. Kaswan is the inventor of Restasis, a medical product for dry eyes, which was approved by the Food and Drug Administration (FDA). I remember mascot owner Sonny Seiler telling me about the product in 1985 when it was used on Uga IV, who had the "painful dry eye condition that can lead to eventual blindness." I knew nothing about it except that Seiler and the family were happy, and it made me happy that I finished my coaching career with one of the greatest Ugas of all time. Neither of us knew at the time that the product would later stir a huge but quiet controversy involving a lawsuit against the University Research Foundation, which was headed by Adams.

In essence, Kaswan claimed that Adams, in order to address budget shortfalls at a time of state funding and to enhance his fund-raising numbers, needed a "quick fix." She reported that he cut a deal for a one-time payment of $22 million in lieu of all royalty payments. Whitt added that the deal "may have lost the University of Georgia more than $200 million in patent revenues."

There were suits and countersuits over the issue for five years, until Superior Court Judge David Sweat in 2007 granted a summary judgment in favor of the Research Foundation, ruling that "Kaswan's contract with the University gives the institution complete control over the patent and [Adams] had the authority to negotiate the deal without informing the inventor." Sweat summarized, "The fact the University made a bad deal... doesn't make it illegal."

Politics and the Attorney General

In *Behind the Hedges,* author Rich Whitt did an in-depth chapter on Georgia Attorney General Thurbert Baker's review of the Deloitte & Touche audit.

In October 2003, shortly after the audit was released to the public, Baker announced that his office was reviewing the report but gave no timetable for a release of any findings. The attorney general's sole responsibility was to determine whether criminal charges should be filed. Despite probing by Whitt and by com-

College Avenue looking north from the UGA campus

petent attorneys familiar with these kinds of investigations, it took the attorney general three and a half years to summarize his report in a letter about the audit.

Whitt was convinced that the "foot dragging" in the matter of the audit was all about politics, and he believed Baker had no desire to "stir the political pot" since his reelection was coming up in 2006. An Emory Law School graduate and the first African American attorney general since the years after the Civil War, Baker was appointed by Democratic Governor Zell Miller to fill the unexpired term of Republican Mike Bowers (UGA Law School 1974), who had resigned in order to run for governor. At that time the state was moving from Democratic to Republican control. Many Democrats saw the handwriting on the wall and switched to the Republican Party. The most notable of these was Governor Sonny Perdue.

As an aside, Perdue, an excellent high school passing quarterback, walked on with the Georgia team in 1965 (my second year). He was part of the superb recruiting class (SEC champions 1966 and 1968) featuring All-Americans and Hall of Famers Bill Stanfill and Jake Scott, along with other great players such as Billy Payne and State Court Judge Kent Lawrence. Perdue chose to give up football in order to prepare himself for admittance to the School of Veterinary Medicine. However, he was proud to be a part of that great recruiting class. In fact, he and his wife, Mary, hosted a reunion party at the mansion for that distinguished 1965 freshman class.

During Roy Barnes's (UGA 1969 AB, 1972 JD) tenure as governor, the Georgia flag (which contained in part the Confederate battle flag) was a hot issue. I made a few calls to key legislators advocating changing the flag. I believed it was the right thing to do, especially considering the many black athletes we had at Georgia. But I was also aware there was a good possibility the NCAA would not allow NCAA-sponsored events in states with blatant racial symbols such as the Georgia flag proved to be at the time. One of the key legislators I called was Perdue, who obviously was taken aback by my call. He would soon be running on a very conservative Republican ticket with the flag as a campaign issue.

Nevertheless, when Perdue became governor, Baker to his credit stood up to the governor in a redistrict-

ing case. Baker, however, had close ties to Miller, being the governor's floor leader helping to guide the HOPE scholarship bill through the House. Thus Whitt contends that with Baker's close ties to Miller, and Miller's relationship with Perdue and Adams, the attorney general's "not searching out new enemies…raises questions as to whether the attorney general took a pass on the Deloitte & Touche report for political reasons."

After three and a half years, Baker wrote the letter mentioned earlier, which Whitt put in his appendix. In summary, Baker found "troubling" things in the report, especially the secret side agreement with Donnan. He was also troubled by the Huckaby honorarium and Adams's salary supplement from the UGA Foundation.

Baker and the attorney general's office denied Whitt's request for an interview after the letter was released. When Whitt asked, "Why did it take three and a half years to write a letter?" the response was, "The letter speaks for itself." Whitt concluded, "It smacks of a cover-up."

Whitt Wrap-Up

Rich Whitt concluded his research in *Behind the Hedges* by devoting a chapter on Regent Don Leebern, followed by conclusions on his exhaustive research. Whitt traced Leebern's ability to shrewdly play both sides of the political spectrum as the tides changed, supporting both Democrats (Zell Miller and Roy Barnes) and Republicans (Sonny Perdue and Nathan Deal.) The "fun-loving" Leebern used his financial generosity, according to Whitt, of "money, liquor, and airplane" to win positions of influence.

While Adams may not have approved of some of Leebern's alleged indiscretions, the president was quoted by Whitt as defending his Regent supporter, saying, "He gets the big issues about as well as anybody I've ever worked with on a board."

As of this writing, Leebern is still on the Board of Regents, and time will tell if the new governor, Nathan Deal, will reappoint him to a fourth term in 2012. Some insiders speculate that because of Leebern's money and his support of Adams, he will be reappointed.

Adams Conclusion

Whitt concluded his book with a chapter on "Conclusions of Adams's Performance." The Pulitzer Prize–investigative reporter gave Adams high marks as a builder, citing such projects as the Paul D. Coverdell Center for Biomedical and Health Research, the Zell Miller Student Learning Center, and the $43-million Special Collections Library. Credit must also be given to Adams for the partnership he negotiated with the Augusta Medical Center to establish a new medical school at the University. Since Whitt's writing, Adams successfully led the charge for an expanded engineering program.

On the other hand, Whitt concluded that Adams, with a reputation for fund-raising, "underperformed in that category," citing as a source the New York–based Council on Aid to Education. "UGA lost ground to other schools in raising money from private sources," the report concluded. It was pointed out that when Adams arrived, UGA's endowment was exceeded only by those of Vanderbilt and Florida in the Southeast. "Since then, Georgia has fallen behind Kentucky, Tennessee, and Arkansas, and remains well below Florida and Vanderbilt," the report added.

While Whitt concluded that Adams "underperformed" in raising money for the University, he pointed out that Adams has "done quite well for himself, doubling his total compensation in the first seven years." Meanwhile, Whitt pointed out that even Adams acknowledged, "UGA has lost ground on faculty salaries and has not kept up with southern research universities." As of 2008, Georgia ranked thirteenth out of sixteen Southern states in the percentage of growth in salaries at top-tier universities.

Whitt spoke to Adams's leadership and his character, calling such an evaluation as being "the most subjective." However, Whitt pointed out, "It says something when under-the-table contracts are kept secret, when petty financial manipulations and habitual obfuscation becomes routine, and when loyalty to the individual is demanded above loyalty to the institution."

Whitt also accused Adams (perhaps unfairly) of personally replacing every academic dean. Whitt stated that all of the deans "he replaced went quietly," except John Soloski, the very capable former dean of the Grady College of Journalism and Mass Communications. Soloski was forced to resign after being accused of sexual harassment. Soloski sued on the basis that he was not allowed to defend himself and that "Adams had used the sexual harassment allegation to punish him for refusing (in 2003) to write a letter calling for an end to the controversy between Adams and the Foundation." Soloski's lawsuit claims the intent of the letter "was to rebuild Adams's ailing credibility in the eyes of the public and the University community."

Soloski won the suit in December 2008, when Judge Christopher Hagy called the University's findings of sexual harassment "a gross abuse of discretion." Soloski's name has been cleared by the University, and today he is teaching in the journalism school. Most all of Adams detractors see the episode as another act of the president's "pettiness."

Atlanta public relations executive Bob Hope said, according to Whitt, "If there ever is a Heisman Trophy for pettiness, Mike Adams would win it and there won't be a second place."

Despite it all, Adams is still very much on his feet and has the backing of the powers that be as he heads into 2012, gearing up for another capital campaign with an estimated goal of $1 billion.

As Adams started the 2011–2012 academic year, he was greeted by a student enrollment of 34,846, the second-largest and perhaps the best-qualified group in the history of the University. The students are a welcome sight to the football team and, for that matter, the entire athletic program, which is recommitted to a "new beginning" after suffering through one of the worst years in Georgia's athletics history that began with a tragic 2010 Fourth of July weekend.

New College and the Chapel with Candler Hall in the background behind old Herty Field

DESPAIR AND HOPE

The Bulldog Nation woke up the morning of July 1, 2010, with the startling news that Athletic Director Damon Evans had been arrested and charged with DUI. In a press conference Evans apologized for his actions and might have saved his job, but when the full report of the incident was released, he had to resign. The police report revealed that Evans was stopped while driving under the influence with an apparent unruly female whose underwear was found in his lap.

I was saddened and felt sorry for both Evans and his family. I had recruited Evans and brought him back to Georgia as the senior associate athletic director for internal affairs. He was smart and talented and had a bright future. He was regarded as a role model African American on a fast track to become whatever he resolved to be. He had vast experience in NCAA matters, serving on every important NCAA committee. He received high marks for his work and was well respected throughout the country.

I had quietly supported Evans to succeed me, but I was hoping to stay on at the University a few more years for him to gain more experience. My support, however, carried the caveat that Claude Felton, our senior associate athletic director for external affairs and our communications director, be

Greg McGarity

graduates with advanced degrees in sports administration, but they lacked experience, and none had ever coached. While they were good "bottom line" administrators, they lacked good experience in human relations. It didn't take long for the morale in the department to plummet.

The tough bottom-line business approach also affected the coaching staff. While I will be the first to admit there was room for retrenchment and belt tightening in the department, the manner in which it was carried out had a demoralizing effect on the coaches. I was once again put in an awkward situation. I wanted to support the new regime, but I did not want to appear as the meddling "old coach and athletic director." So I kept my distance and kept my concerns to myself.

Evans, who has handled his situation admirably, can make amends and get back into athletics if he wants, but it is going to take a while. I will help him all I can. As of this writing, he has a good job in Boston, his wife's hometown. It has been a tough wake-up call, and I know he will learn and grow from the ordeal. I want the best for him.

Evans is also serving in a consulting position with Savannah State, which might mark the beginning of his return to intercollegiate athletics administration.

Greg McGarity: A Bulldog Comes Back Home

The one positive result of the Evans tragedy is that it opened the door for the return of Greg McGarity to his hometown of Athens and his alma mater. When I arrived at the University in 1964 as the head football coach, McGarity was ten years old. He assisted Coach Dan Magill by "sweeping, rolling, and watering" the old rubico tennis courts.

McGarity graduated from the University in 1977 and was serving as a graduate assistant in the department when Athletic Director Joel Eaves hired him as the women's tennis coach. He also doubled as assistant sports information director under Coach Magill. In 1982, I appointed him travel and game manager, and he later became assistant athletic director. In 1992 he became the top assistant at Florida under new Gators athletic director Jeremy Foley. McGarity and Foley had

his number-one assistant and give Evans the benefit of his experience and maturity. That assumption was not to be. In fact, Evans told me that of all the staff members Adams had suggested replacing, Felton was at the top of the list. The president apparently blamed Felton for many of the unflattering articles that had been written about him. Adams, of course, did not think he was responsible for his bad publicity.

Evans was smart enough *not* to get rid of one of the best and most respected communications directors in the country. He did, however, reduce Felton's role to the single but important responsibility of communications director. In turn, he made the mistake, in my opinion, of completely surrounding himself with young Turks who were all cut from the same cloth. They were

Tailgating at UGA

become good friends over the years while working in the same capacity, coordinating the details each year for the Georgia-Florida game in Jacksonville.

McGarity, an energetic, thoughtful, loyal, and solid person of good character, brings a world of experience to the program. He is a Bulldog, happy to be back home, and the right man at the right time for the program. His return has raised the morale in the department tenfold. The future of Georgia athletics is bright! However, the ultimate determination of a successful athletic program rests with the success of the football program. As of this writing, the football team has been struggling, and a lot

of work needs to be done to bring the joy back to the Bulldog Nation.

Georgia Football and Basketball: Success and Failure

As in all athletic competition, as well as all aspects of life, there is success and failure, but neither is final. Coach Mark Richt has provided sterling leadership to the Georgia program. He is a family man of deep faith and solid character, with integrity at the forefront. He

Coach Mark Fox

has also given the Bulldog program championship football, guiding teams to the top of the Southeastern Conference in 2002 and 2005. His 2003 team was the Eastern Division champion. At the start of the 2011 season, Richt has won ten or more games six times during his ten years at Georgia, with a record of 96–34, a winning percentage of .747, ranking him fourth in the nation among the winningest active football bowl subdivision coaches. He also has won consistently from two of the Bulldogs' "archrivals": Georgia Tech (9–1) and Auburn (6–4.) However, his record against Florida (3–8) and season records in 2009 (8–5) and 2010 (6–7) caused unrest in the Bulldog Nation.

This is the first time Richt has gone through some tough times, but it comes with the territory, and every coach has to face crises on and off the field. I certainly had my difficult times, not to mention the likes of "Bear" Bryant and Joe Paterno, who also had struggling times during their careers. I am confident Coach Richt is determined and resolute to address the crisis and will be a better coach in the long run. He got a good start with landing one of the best recruiting classes in the nation in 2011, the so-called dream team. He has also made some staffing changes that will strengthen the program. I would be surprised if there is not significant improvement during the 2011 season. As this book goes to press, I am proud to say Georgia is 8–2, having won eight games in a row (including Florida and Auburn) and is highly favored to win the SEC East title.

Meanwhile, the future of Georgia's other revenue profitable sport, men's basketball, is bright under the leadership of Mark Fox. He took his team to the NCAA tournament in 2011. Fox has been well received by the Georgia people both on and off the court. Fox replaced Dennis Felton who gave the Bulldogs some great moments of glory, the greatest coming in 2009, when his team won the Southeastern Conference basketball tournament as the lowest seed in the history of the league to ever win the championship. Ironically, because of a tornado that damaged the Atlanta Dome during the tournament, the competition site was shifted to the Georgia Tech Arena, where the Bulldogs won the championship. However, the following year, Felton's team won 12 and lost 20, and Evans replaced him with Fox.

With the ups and downs of Georgia athletics and the changing of personnel over the many years, there is one small group of Bulldog trumpeters that have remained constant as athletics closes in on its 126th year of existence. In 2012, baseball (the Bulldogs oldest sport, which started in 1886) and football (which started in 1892) will celebrate their 126th and 120th birthdays, respectively.

Georgia's "big three" living historians and my longtime friends and advisors Dan Magill, (the nation's greatest Bulldog at 90+!) Loran Smith, and Claude Felton continue to write and support the "Dawgs!" Their combined experience in covering and writing about Bulldog athletics and its history spans almost 150 years. All have served the University Athletic Association in the sports information office and have written many books and articles on the Bulldogs' many athletic programs. There is no institution in America that can boast of having three such competent and devoted athletic historians as these three men. Their loyalty and devotion to Georgia has kept alive the Bulldog spirit in the best and worst of times.

Athletic Budget

Football and men's basketball at UGA are the only two sports that earn a profit. In round numbers, it is estimated that football funds over 85 percent of the budget. As of 2011–2012, that is almost $90 million. Thanks to television revenue, men's basketball turns a profit, and the basketball revenue, combined with the other sports (primarily baseball and women's gymnastics), brings in the remaining 15 percent of the budgeted funds.

A June 16, 2011, article in *USA Today* listed Georgia as ninth among the ten top schools nationally that produce net revenue. Georgia's net revenue in 2009–2010 was $9,282,558, and the bulk of surplus revenues usually goes toward capital improvements, University grants, reserves, and escalating coaches' salaries (a challenging issue in intercollegiate athletics).

Coach Mark Richt's salary is listed at approximately $2.8 million, with incentives that could reach $3.3 million. Gene Chizik, the Auburn coach who won the National Championship in 2010, is now making $3.2 million, with incentives that could earn him $4.5 million. But the highest paid coaches are Nick Saban at Alabama (annual salary over $4.1 million plus incentives) and Mack Brown at Texas (annual salary $4.2

Loran Smith and Larry Munson

million—slightly higher than Saban's).

Whenever my wife, Barbara, reads about the salaries of coaches, she gets mad, repeating what she has said numerous times: "Why would you work twenty-five years, finally start making some money [my last year's total income as both athletic director and head football coach in 1988 was $500,000] and quit?" The answer, of course, is *it's not all about money*!

I still have my first contract framed on a wall in the office. It is a one-page, three-paragraph contract that starts with the "party of the first part" and lists my salary at $12,000 with a $2,500 subsistence. Not listed was a $1,000 statewide weekly television coach's show supplement I had negotiated with the old C&S Bank, bringing my total package to $15,500! I remember someone quipped at the time that this amount was "just about what you were worth when you came," and it probably was. I was happy for the opportunity.

Uga VI

Band and Cheerleaders

In addition to scholarships, a special part of the budget for me has always been the band and cheerleaders who reward the Bulldog Nation with their colorful spirit. The UGA Athletic Association band budget for 2011–2012 is $630,000, which covers scholarships, travel, uniforms, etc. This amount does not cover the band at bowl games, which is budgeted separately and funded by bowl revenue.

The Georgia Redcoats are over a hundred years old, going all the way back to 1905, when the band consisted of some twenty to thirty members and operated as part of the military department. Some 107 years later, the Redcoats total over 350 members, including the Georgettes and the Flag Line.

I have always felt a deep affection and appreciation for this unified, hardworking group, especially when I was coaching. The players use to complain about two-a-day practices in preparation for the season, but I would always point to the band, who in preseason would go *all* day and *all* night in their preseason preparation. A special memory is the Thursday nights before the first game when the Redcoats would have a complete rehearsal, which I always attended since I never saw the show at halftime. After the rehearsal, the band would sit on the field in a circle, and I would visit with them, praising their performance and thanking them for providing the "heartbeat" of the Bulldog spirit for our team, the students, the alumni, and the fans.

The Redcoats rewarded me in 2002 by asking that I be present at the Sutler Awards presentation. The award recognized the "Redcoats as among the elite marching band programs in the country" and the first band in the SEC to win the award. Barbara and I recently spoke at one of their fund-raisers and made a $50,000 contribution for an endowed scholarship.

An equally hardworking group who contributes much to the "spirit of the Dawgs" is the cheerleaders. It was a longtime tradition when I was coaching and then serving as athletic director for Barbara and me to have all the cheerleaders to the house for lasagna prior to the first game. We have some fun photos of those events, and the occasion enabled me to express my appreciation to the cheerleaders and their coaches (Mike Castronis and Mary Lou Braswell) for all they meant to the program.

I still see many of those former cheerleaders from time to time, and it always stirs a lot of memories of their Bulldog spirit and enthusiasm. A special point of cheerleader pride surfaced in 2007 when Natasha Trethewey, captain of the cheerleading squad in 1987, won a Pulitzer Prize for her poem "Native Guard." The poem was about the black Union soldiers during the Civil War who were assigned as guards to the Confederate prison on Ship Island off the coast of Mississippi. I called to congratulate Natasha and found out that she holds the Phyllis Wheatley Distinguished Chair in Poetry at Emory. During our phone visit, I wanted to talk about her poem, but all she wanted to talk about was her cheerleading days. Natasha incidentally is the first UGA graduate outside the journalism profession to win the Pulitzer Prize. Speaking of the Pulitzer Prize, another UGA protégé who also won the prestigious award is Dr. Edward J. Larson.

Multitalented Professor Edward J. Larson

Edward J. Larson, a highly respected historian and legal scholar who once served as the Richard B. Russell Professor of History and Herman E. Talmage Chair of Law, received the Pulitzer Prize for history in 1988. His book *Summer for the Gods: The Scopes Trial and America's Continuing Debate over Science and Religion* concludes that the trial and its legend were just the beginning of "the American struggle between individual liberty and majoritarian democracy." Historian F. N. Boney said of Larson, "Over the years he also earned a reputation as an outstanding teacher, a combination often sought but not so often attained in American higher education." As of 2011, Larson is professor of history at Pepperdine University, where he holds the Hugh and Hazel Darling Chair in Law.

Larson has written another highly regarded and timely book in 2011 published by Yale University Press titled *An Empire on Ice.* The book celebrates the one hundredth anniversary of Robert Scott's and Ernest Shackleton's reaching the South Pole. Larson, who continues to serve as a senior fellow of UGA's Institute of Higher Education, was a valued member of the Athletic Board in 2003–2004 during my last two years as athletic director. His parents are Ohio State graduates, and he received an honorary doctorate in humane letters from that institution in 2004.

Of special interest is *The* Ohio State University, as it is officially and proudly called by Buckeye followers, was listed in the June 2011 article of *USA Today* with Georgia as being in the top twenty "big time schools winning the profit game." There are five schools from the Big 10 and five from the SEC on the list. Only 22 schools out of 120 institutions in Division 1A (now called the Football Bowl Subdivision) are turning a profit. The other subdivisions (IAA, II, and III) all are

losing money. Despite the financial strain of football, institutions continue to have programs, and many more are starting the sport, especially in the South. In fact, by 2010–2011 19 schools have added or reintroduced football on their campuses. Another 17 will add the sport between 2012 and 2014. Many have asked why? The late J. Douglas Toma, professor of higher education at the University of Georgia, appears to have the answer.

J. Douglas Toma: Football U

It was a sad but memorable, if not glorious day in the life of the University when many friends (faculty, staff, and students) gathered on June 10, 2011, to celebrate the life of Professor J. Douglas "Doug" Toma. He had passed away at the age of forty-seven, leaving a wife of fourteen years (Linda) and a seven-year-old son, Jack. With a Michigan State undergraduate degree and PhD and law degrees from Michigan, Toma loved intercollegiate athletics, especially football. He was regarded as one of the leading young scholars in the field, with specialties in the law, policy, structure, and management of colleges and universities.

Toma was one of those rare individuals in the academic community who gained in a short period of time the love and respect of all who knew him. UGA Professor Emeritus and Vice President Emeritus for Instruction Tom Dyer said it best: "He was a colleague's colleague...a fan, a student, a scholar and a friend, personally and professionally."

Toma's book *In Football U: Spectator Sports in the Life of the American University* discusses the strategic uses of college football at research universities. But, as Jeffery Orleans, executive director of the council of the Ivy Group presidents, wrote, "This is a book about education, not sports. Its discussions of the context in which athletics operates—'college life,' and the economics and cultures of major research universities—are required reading for anyone who wants to truly understand the rapidly changing nature of American higher education." The book was a tremendous resource to me in a consulting project, where I drew upon my experience at UGA.

I met Toma shortly after his arrival at the University in 2003. I later spoke to his class while he was dean of UGA's Franklin Residential College. In 2010, I participated with him in the Global LEAD studies-abroad programs in South Africa and Greece. I even had the privilege to speak to the class that he, along with former UGA president Chuck Knapp, conducted for the Institute of Higher Education. The class was for those pursuing a doctorate (EdD) in higher education management.

My topic was leadership and current issues of intercollegiate athletics in higher education. Leadership was discussed in detail, especially as it pertained to the prolonged recession in the state and in the nation. There were examples of individuals' superb leadership during the worst economic times. I referenced, for example, Aflac chairman and CEO Daniel P. Amos (UGA 1973, BBA in risk management) as a classic model of real leadership during difficult times. Amos, who was entitled to a substantial performance bonus in 2009, refused to take the bonus in light of his Aflac employees' suffering from the recession and the drastic reduction in Aflac's stock value.

The strong leadership example of Amos led to a discussion of UGA president Adams's leadership role. At issue was leadership during the crisis of severe state funding cuts and salary freezes (three years) of most all state employers. After much discussion, many in the class, including the class facilitators, felt that Adams passed up an exemplary leadership opportunity. Some suggested it would have been an inspiring leadership example for him to have taken a slight pay cut, thereby sending a message of "feeling the pain" of all the University employees. Adams not only passed on a salary cut opportunity, but a year later, in 2011, he was able to secure a substantial pay increase.

It is surprising that, during a period of severe budget cuts and salary freezes at the University, Adams accepted a $50,000 increase to his deferred compensation. The salary increase was justified by the Regents, based on comparing Adams's salary to President G. P. "Bud" Peterson of Georgia Tech, who was making slightly more but had far less longevity than the UGA president. Peterson, incidentally a nationally regarded scientific academician, was recruited to Georgia Tech in 2009 from the University of Colorado, where he was chancellor.

The $50,000 increase brings Adams's total package

to $661,012, making him the highest-paid president in the state system, surpassing his colleague Peterson, who makes $644,120, according to the March 31, 2011, *Chronicle of Higher Education.* The increase puts Adams's compensation in the upper 12 percent of the 185 public-university chief executives in the nation.

The salary increase was another opportunity to show real leadership in a crisis by turning down the raise, at least temporarily, or perhaps, as someone suggested, designating it to a charity for two years. Instead, Adams accepted the offer in the worst of economic times, subjecting himself to justifiable criticism. *The Red and Black* newspaper the next day, June 16, was critical of Adams for taking a "$50,000 pay increase, even though the University System of Georgia is facing $300 million in state budget cuts." The newspaper continued, "To raise the salary leaves us skeptical as to how in tune President Adams is with the people he is supposed to be leading." The editorial asked, How could Adams "understand the recession's effects on Georgia students and families while he is enjoying the perks of a five figure raise." The same question can be asked by the faculty and staff.

In the same issue of *The Red and Black,* the dean of the College of Veterinary Medicine, Sheila Allen, noted the impact on "morale" of state cutbacks and the fear of losing "more faculty, staff and graduate students." She also worried that "programs could be closed and discontinued."

The vehicle used to pay for Adams's $50,000 increase is through "a new lease agreement," whereby the Georgia Athletic Association would funnel $50,000 in 2011–2012 to the Regents for Adams. The Athletic Association authorized the expenditure in a called meeting of the Executive Committee. However, the full board was never contacted for approval or even informed of this budget amendment.

The longtime lease agreement between the Board of Regents and the UGA Athletic Association has an interesting history. The Athletic Association, after financing, building, and paying for facilities (valued now at well over $190 million—$110 million on Sanford Stadium alone), turns all of the properties over to the Board of Regents, who in turn courteously agreed to lease the facilities back to the Athletic Association for $1 a year. It is this lease agreement, which has been in existence

Uga VII

for several decades, that has been changed by the Regents (with the compliance of the Athletic Association) that will be used to increase Adams's pay.

The rationale for using athletic money is to avoid the appropriation of tax funds. While the Athletic Association funds may not come from the state's public funds, the money does come from the public funds of Bulldog supporters.

Toma's Book: A Shining Light

Toma's book *In Football U* was a guiding light for me in my consultant work with Kennesaw State University during the study of the possibilities of starting a football program at the institution. Ironically, Kennesaw State University (KSU) was officially founded as a junior college in 1963, the same year I became football coach at UGA. To the surprise of many, KSU had an enrollment of 24,500 in the fall semester of 2011.

Few, if any, professors with the academic prestige of Toma ever attempted to perform such controversial research on the value of spectator sports (especially football) to public universities. Because Toma was so well respected, many have taken notice. My extensive use of his research in my work at Kennesaw State provided broad credibility to the study. The following is a sampling of my findings and its ties to UGA.

From the beginning of the study at Kennesaw State it was generally assumed that the greatest challenge of starting football would be financial. This assumption was confirmed and further reinforced by the fact that only 20 percent of the established football programs in the country are profitable. The football cost challenge is also escalated by the demands of Title IX compliance and the accompanying need to have a school band. It is obvious, however, that those institutions that are playing football, and the many institutions that have just started or soon will start football (twenty-five by 2014, mainly in the South), are convinced that the many tangible and intangible benefits outweigh the financial challenges of adding the sport.

However, there are other challenges centered on the high visibility and popularity of the sport. There is constant danger that excesses could and have led to scandals for institutions. While the number of programs cited as rule violators are small compared to the total numbers, and the number of athletes that have stained their program are very small compared to the total number of participants, the incidents are a source of gross embarrassment. Alleged serious NCAA violations make huge headlines. It is reassuring that the NCAA, under the leadership of President Mark Emmert, has been committed to stiffer penalties on recent violations by institutions, players, coaches, and administrators. Despite the challenges, institutions believe the risks are worth the rewards.

Several schools (like Kennesaw State) have constructed on-campus housing, dining, and fitness facilities. Those schools perceive starting football as the natural next step in changing their reputations from commuter-based institutions to residential universities conducive to a more vibrant campus life. This transformation no doubt will help attract accomplished students, boost alumni interaction, and encourage potential new donor support as it has done at the University of Georgia. Football will also help bring community leaders and state legislators to these campuses, potentially increasing their exposure and support just as it has done for decades at UGA. All of those resources will help maintain and grow the institution.

Historically, football has defined the unique culture of an institution through its proud band (Redcoats), colors (red and black), mascot (Bulldogs), songs ("Glory, Glory"), and traditions (tailgating, the chapel bell, between the hedges, the oval G, and How 'Bout Them Dawgs!). In addition, football provides a university a "national brand," giving distinction and national prominence to UGA and other institutions not readily available in other avenues of the campus.

Lastly, football provides a sense of pride and a point of connection to a broad audience of supporters in the community and around the state. Certainly across the nation, universities that have football and marching bands have a more energized campus life, as those activities have served as the heartbeat of tradition and student life.

Toma has confirmed what UGA historian F. N. Boney has been contending for years: that football and agriculture education were major factors in transforming the University of Georgia from a "very small all white, all male, liberal arts school for a very few privileged kids to...a real people's school." "Football fans," Boney said, "popped up all over the state and many who never got near the campus rooted for the Dawgs!" As Toma wrote, "They come to think of the institution as their own."

This "real people's school" at UGA embraces all 159 counties of the largest state east of the Mississippi. Georgia enters its 227th year since the signing of the charter on January 27, 1785, that created the first chartered state public university in America. This institution that so many feel "is their own" continues to make history as it steadfastly pursues its revised motto, "To teach, to serve, and to inquire into the nature of things." The University has done and will continue to do that very well, always striving for perfection.

I have two academic degrees from Auburn, as does my wife, Barbara. Three of my children have UGA undergraduate degrees, and one son (the head football coach at Tennessee) is a Georgia Law School graduate. And with nine descendants still to go, I have two grandchildren who have degrees from Alabama and Vanderbilt. But with all the "outside" influences, I still bleed red and black and always will. So it's "Glory, glory to ole Georgia," past, present, and future, and I am proud to have played a small role in this story.

$\mathcal{S}$OURCES

Books

Avary, Myrta Lockett. *Recollections of Alexander H. Stephens.* Baton Rouge, Louisiana: Louisiana State University Press, 1998. 572. Print.

Boney, F. N. *A Pictorial History of the University of Georgia.* Athens, Georgia: University of Georgia Press, 1984. 302. Print.

Boney, F. N. *A Walking Tour of the University of Georgia.* Athens, Georgia: University of Georgia Press, 1989. 97. Print.

Brown, Barry L., and Gordon R. Elwell. *Crossroads of Conflict: A Guide to Civil War Sites in Georgia.* Athens, Georgia: University of Georgia Press, 2010. 245. Print.

Coulter, E. Merton. *College Life in the Old South.* Athens, Georgia: Macmillan Company, 1983. 320. Print.

Dyer, Thomas G. *The University of Georgia: A Bicentennial History.* Athens, Georgia: University of Georgia Press, 1985. 435. Print.

Evans, David. *Sherman's Horsemen.* Bloomington, Indiana: Indiana University Press, 1999. 645. Print.

Gurr, Charles Stephen. *The Personal Equation: A Biography of Steadman Vincent Sanford.* Athens, Georgia: University of Georgia Press, 1999. 264. Print.

Henson, Allen Lumpkin. *Red Galluses: A Story of Georgia Politics.* Boston, Massachusetts: Active Printing, Co., 1945. 269. Print.

Kirby, James. *Fumble: Bear Bryant, Wally Butts and the Great College Football Scandal.* Orlando, Florida: Harcourt Brace Jovanovich, 1986. 248. Print.

Reap, James K. *Athens: A Pictorial History.* Norfolk, Virginia: The Donning Company, 1985. 208. Print.

Smith, Loran. *Between the Hedges: 100 Years of Georgia Football.* Marietta, Georgia: Longstreet Press, Inc., 1992. 227. Print.

Smithgall, Lessie. *I Took the Fork.* Marietta, Georgia: Mana Publications, Inc., 2008. 203. Print.

Stanford, Henry King. *Campus Under Political Fire and Other Essays*. Columbus, Georgia: X-Press Printing, 1968. 208. Print.

Stegeman, John F. *The Ghosts of Herty Field*. Athens, Georgia: University of Georgia Press, 1997. 147. Print.

Stegeman, John F., and Robert M. Willingham, Jr. *Touchdown: A Pictorial History of the Georgia Bulldogs*. Athens, Georgia: Agee Publishers, Inc., 166. Print.

Stephens, Lester D. Joseph LeConte: Gentle Prophet of Evolution. Baton Rouge, LA: Louisiana State University Press, 1982. 340. Print.

Thomas, Frances Taliaferro. *A Portrait of Historic Athens & Clarke County*. Second. Athens, Georgia: University of Georgia Press, 1992. 334. Print.

Thurmond, Michael L. *Freedom: An African-American History of Georgia, 1733-1865*. 2002. Print.

Toma, J. Douglas. *Football U: Spectator Sports in the Life of the American University*. University of Michigan Press, 2006. 292. Print.

Whitt, Rich. *Behind the Hedges*. Montgomery, Alabama: NewSouth Books, 2009. 288. Print.

Younts, Gene. *Alive As Long As He Lived: The Story of John William Fanning*. Thompson-Shore, Inc., 2002. 322. Print.

Publications

Adams, Michael F. "The 2011 State of the University." Columns. (2011): 4. Print.

Allison, Jim. "A Dynasty of Georgia Naturalists." *Tipularia*. 25. (2010): 8. Print.

Berkowitz, Steve, and Jodi Upton. "Money Flows to College Sports." *USA Today* June 16, 2011: 1. Print.

Brubaker, Bill. "Minimum Standard, Maximum Dispute." *Washington Post* July 25, 1999, Print.

Graham, Jr. Frank. "The Story of a College Football Fix." Saturday Evening Post. March 23, 1963: 4. Print.

Jones, Barry W. "Agriculture History." Athens, Georgia, 2004.

Jones, Dr. Barry, and Dr. David Knauft. University of Georgia College of Agriculture and Environmental Sciences. Conner Hall: The First One Hundred Years. Athens, 2008. Print.

Magill, Dan. "The Pick of Dan Magill." (1999): 54. Print.

Magill, Dan. "The Pick of Dan Magill." V. (2009): 30. Print.

Magill, Dan. "The Pick of Dan Magill's Columns." IV. (2009): 30. Print.

Marinova, Polina. "Vet School Dean Fears More Cuts." *Red & Black* June 16, 2011, Vol. 118, No. 142: 1. Print.

Mohlenbrock, Robert H. "The Magic Rock Garden." *Natural History*. April 2009: 2. Print.

Shearer, Lee. "$50,000 Pay Boost for UGA President." *Athens Banner Herald* June 15, 2011, Vol. 179, No. 166: 1. Print.

Wicker, Wesley K. *Of Time and Place: The Presidential Odyssey of Dr. Henry King Stanford*. Unpublished doctorial dissertation. Athens, Georgia: 1990. Print.

"www.senate.gov/artandhistory." N.p., n.d. Web. 27 Jun 2011.

2010 Georgia Football Media Guide